MY LIFE,
AS I SEE IT

ALSO BY DIONNE WARWICK

My Point of View

Say a Little Prayer (coauthor)

MY LIFE, AS I SEE IT

An Autobiography

DIONNE WARWICK

WITH DAVID FREEMAN WOOLEY

ATRIA BOOKS

New York   London   Toronto   Sydney

ATRIA BOOKS

A Division of Simon & Schuster, Inc.
1230 Avenue of the Americas
New York, NY 10020

First Atria Books hardcover edition November 2010

ATRIA BOOKS and colophon are trademarks of Simon & Schuster, Inc.

For information about special discounts for bulk purchases,
please contact Simon & Schuster Special Sales at
1-866-506-1949 or business@simonandschuster.com.

The Simon & Schuster Speakers Bureau can bring authors
to your live event. For more information or to book an event,
contact the Simon & Schuster Speakers Bureau at
1-866-248-3049 or visit our website at www.simonspeakers.com.

Designed by Dana Sloan

Manufactured in the United States of America

10   9   8   7   6   5   4   3   2   1

Library of Congress Cataloging-in-Publication Data

Warwick, Dionne.
    My life, as I see it : an autobiography / by Dionne Warwick with David Freeman Wooley.
        p.   cm.
    Includes index.
    1. Warwick, Dionne.   2. Singers—United States—Biography.   I. Wooley, David Freeman.   II. Title.
ML420.W195A3   2010
782.42164092—dc22[B]   2010032852

ISBN 978-1-4391-7134-9
ISBN 978-1-4391-7136-3 (ebook)

This book is dedicated to my entire family,
my two sons,
and all six of my grandchildren.
—Dionne

The Lord is my shepherd; I shall not want.
—Psalm 23

CONTENTS

———————

MY LIFE,
AS I SEE IT

CHAPTER 1

If You Can Think It, You Can Do It

WHEN MY grandfather, the Reverend Elzae Warrick, asked me to sing at his church, the St. Luke's AME Church in Newark, New Jersey, one Sunday morning, I was truly surprised. As I entered his pulpit, I looked up at him, wondering why he wanted me to sing. He simply said, "Sing for me the song you sing in Sunday school." I was only six years old, and this would be the first time I would sing in front of a large congregation of people. Grandpa could see that I was a bundle of nerves and leaned down to whisper, "Remember, if you can think it, you can do it."

He then stacked a few books beside the pulpit for me to stand on, so everybody could see me. I closed my eyes as tight as I could, said a quick prayer, and then started to sing:

> *Jesus loves me, this I know,*
> *For the Bible tells me so.*
> *Little ones to Him belong,*

They are weak, but He is strong.
Yes, Jesus loves me!
Yes, Jesus loves me!
Yes, Jesus loves me!
The Bible tells me so.

Midway through, I found the courage to open one eye a little bit. The people in the congregation were smiling and urging me on. They were shouting, "Sing that song," "Take your time," and "Amen."

Me at six years old: No, I did not want to take this photo.
(Personal collection of Dionne Warwick)

Their encouragement seemed to wash over me, and I began to feel more confident. I closed my eyes again and really started to let loose. Even I was amazed at what was coming out of my little mouth and the notes I was able to hit. The moment was truly magical.

When I finished, I opened my eyes and was amazed to see the entire congregation on their feet. I had received my first standing ovation.

I DID IT then— and after fifty years in show business, I'm still doing it now.

I was born Marie Dionne Warrick on December 12, 1940, and raised in East Orange, New Jersey, where my mommy, Lee Drinkard Warrick, my daddy, Mancel L. Warrick, my sister, Delia "Dee Dee" Warrick, and my brother, Mancel "Pookie" Warrick Jr., lived comfortably in a two-family home that we owned.

I was named Marie after my mother's sister. My godmother, Dezbe, chose Dionne as my middle name. The only person ever to call me Marie was my gym teacher, Ms. Perry. That fact helped me to recognize her name when—what seemed like a hundred years later—she sent a note to me backstage at a performance in Florida. It was addressed to Marie. I was not only able to know that she was there, I announced her presence to the audience and told them that she calls me Marie and why. She looked exactly the same as I had remembered: she had the greatest haircut; it's called an Italian bob, and she still wears her silver-gray hair the exact same way, short and always neat.

I was lucky to have good teachers and two wonderful parents who were brought up in God-fearing families and who raised their children in a similar fashion. I had what was considered a normal childhood at that time, in a neighborhood full of families much like

My grandfather, the Reverend Elzae Warrick (seated, center),
and the St. Luke's AME Senior Choir.
(Personal collection of Dionne Warwick)

mine, with a mother and father who gave us love and discipline in major proportions.

My father's father was a minister—he was also one of the wisest men ever to walk this earth, second only to Jesus, in my mind.

Attending church was an important part of life for my mother's side of the family as well. That part of my family was full of gospel singers. Spending the entire day in church every Sunday was not exactly what we children ever wanted to do, but that's what happened. Our folks wouldn't have it any other way.

My mother was a five-foot-four-inch bundle of energy, stylish, and, although soft-spoken, could put the fear of God in you with just a look. She worked at an electrical plant called Tung-Sol in Newark, New Jersey. She made filaments for lightbulbs, and I don't think she ever missed a day of work. I believe this taught us the worth of responsibility and the importance of earning your way through life. This was especially significant given there were not many role models for women who aspired to careers and work of their own at that time. The word I most associate with my mother is *class*. This captures the image of her that Dee Dee and I both kept of her and followed.

Mommy expressed the importance of being a "lady" at all times in the ways we dressed, walked, spoke, and presented ourselves to the world. I sure hope that I have maintained the legacy she gave us.

My daddy stood a full foot taller than my mom did. He was six foot four, lean, and gorgeous. He worked for the railroad as a Pullman porter, one of the best jobs available to African American men

That's my dad.
(Personal collection of Dionne Warwick)

in his time. His legacy for us included an entrepreneurial spirit and vocal ability as well. He had a wonderful voice. When he retired from the railroad, he decided to become a certified public accountant. He took a correspondence course that earned him certification. As a consequence, he became my personal accountant. He also had a career after retirement as a butcher, a candy store owner, and, finally, a gospel record promoter for Hob Records. He also wrote a book, *The Progress of Gospel Music,* published by Vantage Press in 1977, and was on the road with me for a while as my road manager. So my daddy gave me that "get up and go" spirit. I was also a real daddy's girl.

We lived at 46 Sterling Street in a large two-family house. We rented the first floor of our house to the Stewards, who were much like an extended part of our family. Frank and Henrine were parents like mine, who lovingly raised George, Frank Jr., Gwendolyn, and Bobby. We did practically everything together: went to the same schools, shared birthday celebrations and arguments. Gwen and I took piano lessons together every Wednesday after school from Mrs. Giggetts, the organist at my grandfather's church, and we became quite good. Gwen and I even performed at piano recitals that made Mrs. Giggetts, our parents, and our neighbors proud. Gwen was older than I was; however, she was my best friend.

After my brother, Pookie, was born, we moved right next door, to 44 Sterling. Our new home was a bit larger, with five bedrooms, three bathrooms, a living room, a dining room, and a bigger kitchen. Dee Dee and I had our own bedrooms, so we had privacy—as if we needed it. The only other differences were that we now had a large porch area and a large lawn in front of the house. We also had a German shepherd named Sonny Boy. Our lives there were full of happy, fun-filled times.

Because I could hit a baseball, catch a football, play basketball, shoot marbles, and play street hockey as well as most of the boys on Sterling Street, I was considered a tomboy, but I was also very prissy. I loved wearing frilly dresses, jumping rope, having my hair curled, and playing with makeup like any other little girl. I had the best of both worlds rolled into one little body.

Our neighborhood resembled the United Nations. Every race, color, creed, and religion lived on our block. Every parent knew one another, and the friendships I made then are still a very important part of my life. We walked to school together and had sleepovers at each other's homes. We played all kinds of games, including jacks and double Dutch jump rope. Some were games of skill and others were educational, such as Scrabble, spelling bees, and our version of what is now known as *Jeopardy!* We all went to a park called "the Oval," where baseball, tennis, track meets, and other sporting events were held and taught by caring adults.

One of the most important things our family did was to sit down together for dinner. We had wonderful conversations at the dinner table about a variety of topics, including show business.

As I look back, I had a wonderful family life that got even better when my aunt Cissy came to live with us after my grandfather (my mother's father) passed. Though Cissy, whose real first name is Emily, is my mother's younger sister, she is only seven years older than I am. So while she was technically our aunt, she became like our big sister and lived with us until she got married. Aunt Cissy would later give birth to a little girl who would become one of the great voices of our time, my cousin Whitney Houston.

My mom and her sisters, Cissy, Marie ("Rebie"), and Annie, and her brothers, Nick and Larry, all had great voices and at the time performed as the Drinkard Jubilairs. They would later be-

The young Drinkard Jubilairs, with (left to right)
Nick, Annie, Rebie, Larry, and Cissy.
(Personal collection of Dionne Warwick)

come the Drinkard Singers. They held rehearsals in our living room, and since they could be heard up and down Sterling Street, the entire neighborhood got to share these wonderful times—and their singing.

The Drinkard Singers were a fabulous family gospel group, and Mommy was one of its founding members. They made quite a name for themselves and were part of the cavalcade of gospel groups that regularly toured the country. My maternal grandfather, Nitch

Drinkard, was one of the keys to the group's success. He considered gospel singing a ministry and the Drinkard Singers a way to spread the message of Jesus Christ to the masses.

They had begun singing down in Savannah, Georgia, where they lived in the late 1930s. The family, like so many other African Americans, eventually moved north. Cissy joined them when she was just a young thing, probably around five or six years old. Mommy became the group's manager, in addition to her work at Tung-Sol. Every now and then, I would sing with them.

In 1951 they were one of the first groups to accompany the great Mahalia Jackson at a groundbreaking concert at Carnegie Hall, and in 1957 they, along with Mahalia and a few other gospel groups, including Clara Ward and the Ward Singers, performed at George Wein's Newport Jazz Festival. That was the first time the festival featured gospel music. The performance was recorded and became a live album, *The Drinkard Singers and the Back Home Choir at Newport*. The Drinkard Singers were so successful at Newport that RCA Records signed them, making them the first gospel group signed by the label. *A Joyful Noise* was their first studio album, released in 1958.

Our family practically expected that Dee Dee, Pookie, and I would follow in their footsteps. And that almost became a reality. Both Dee Dee and I enjoyed professional singing careers, but my brother, as it is said, "couldn't hold a tune in a paper bag." No, Pookie could not sing, nor did he want to. He had other things on his mind. He became an excellent baseball player, scouted by former Brooklyn Dodger Big Don "Newk" Newcombe, one of the first African American pitchers in the major leagues and a friend of my father. Pookie pleased my parents otherwise by becoming the first to marry and present them with their first grandchild, Barrance D. Warrick. Barry grew up to be quite a sound engineer. He started

My brother, Mancel "Pookie" Warrick, and his son, Barrance.
(Personal collection of Dionne Warwick)

doing my sound in live performances and then on the road with
Burt Bacharach, subsequently doing sound for various TV shows
including *American Idol, Jimmy Kimmel Live!*, the Grammy Awards,
and *Late Night with Conan O'Brien.* I know that his dad, who made
his transition following an automobile accident in 1968, would be
busting buttons with pride just as his mother, fortunately, continues
to do.

The encouragement my parents, grandparents, and all in our
church gave me that first time I sang before an audience gave me
the formula that I have used to support and push my own family. I
have raised them to believe that their dreams can become a reality. I
say to them what my grandfather said to me: "If you can think it,
you can do it." I try to practice it in my daily life even today.

When I was growing up in the late 1940s and early 1950s, African American youngsters didn't have a whole lot of options when it came to jobs and formal education. In those days, it was a huge achievement for any family, especially an African American family, to send a son or daughter off to college.

Back in East Orange, we learned that if you worked hard in school, you could achieve your goals and make your dreams come true. Our intelligence and ambition were encouraged by our family and community. Consequently, many of us went on to college. And when we graduated, we were doctors, lawyers, teachers, scientists, government employees, professors, actors and actresses, and entertainers.

My education started at the Lincoln Grammar School, now renamed the Dionne Warwick Institute of Economics and Entrepreneurship; continued at the Vernon L. Davey Junior High School, now the Cecily Tyson Performing Arts School; and at the East Orange High School, all in East Orange. I went on to the Hartt College of Music in West Hartford, Connecticut, where I earned my bachelor's degree in music education and later returned for my master's degree in music.

During my early school years, I was inspired by many of my teachers. One who remains vividly in my mind is my third-grade teacher, Mrs. Daniels, because she made me understand the meaning of the word *can*.

In class one day, I repeatedly said, "I can't do this." As a consequence, she asked me to come to the front of the class and had me write a word on the blackboard. She asked me to write the word *American* in this manner: "AMER—I—CAN." She asked me what the word was, and I answered, and then she asked me to pronounce the word as it was written. I did. And then she asked if I saw an apostrophe or a *t* anywhere in what I had written. Of course I answered no, and it became clear to me the I-CAN part of the word was what she wanted me to understand. The word *can't* to this very day does not exist in any part of my vocabulary, and I have passed this on to my children and grandchildren. And they all understand that "I can" is the phrase they should live by. And now I am passing that on to you.

A multitude of friends and family made growing up pretty easy for me. In fact, the first rough spot I recall hitting was when I developed a crush on a guy named Virgil.

First of all, Virgil was considered an older young man—all of eighteen. I was fourteen at the time. The reaction of my friends and my parents meant that I had to be content to "moon" over Virgil from afar. He never knew any different.

I was seventeen when I had my first real boyfriend, Jackie Martin, with whom I became engaged while he was in the service. I just knew he was my true love; that is, until I met Bill Elliott.

During my high school years, I was a candy striper, a member of the gospel chorus and the glee club, and had the distinguished pleasure of being chosen to sing in the prestigious New Jersey All-State Choir, a group that anyone who thought they could hold a tune wanted to join.

Auditions were competitive and the elimination process grueling. All this made receiving that letter of acceptance all the more joyous for my family and me. The choir performed a concert in Atlantic City. We were seniors in high school staying in a hotel on our own for the first time. We shared rooms, of course, and were supervised—but we felt like adults. The experience, including the concert, was glorious and will always be one of the highlights of my life.

SINGING WASN'T the only vision I had for my future. Remembering what Grandpa had said to me, I wanted to be many things.

I aspired to be a ballerina. I loved their dignity and grace, some of which I try to convey in my stage show. I thought of being a court stenographer—I was always curious and perhaps a little nosy as a child. The thought of being a teacher became the most interesting to me, and I still feel I can share with others some of what I have learned. But it was the pursuit of a music career that propelled my sister, Dee Dee, and me to start our own gospel group, the Gospelaires, in 1957. And that's when things started to take off.

We were still in high school, but we could sing our little hearts out. Besides Dee Dee and me, there were Myrna Utley, her brother John, Carol Slade, and Sylvia Shemwell. We were all members of the New Hope Baptist Church and the C. H. Walters Choir. Reverend C. H. Walters was pastor of New Hope. Myrna and Sylvia became members of the Sweet Inspirations along with Estelle Brown and my aunt Cissy, who founded the group. They went on to be very successful.

Singing at church functions and gospel caravans, we began to make a name for ourselves throughout the state of New Jersey and other parts of the eastern seaboard. Our efforts were promoted by our church members, friends, and, of course, the Drinkard Singers. We Gospelaires felt that we were carrying on the legacy given to us by the Drinkard Singers to spread the word of our Heavenly Father through song.

We ultimately felt strong enough to compete at the world-renowned Apollo Theater in Harlem, New York, during one of its gospel shows, in which the Drinkards were appearing with other renowned gospel singers. The amateur talent contests at the theater have always been legend. The audiences have long enjoyed a reputation for being tough, smart, and unafraid to let you know how they really feel about your performance. The amateur night is a Wednesday-night tradition that started way back in 1934, and Ella

Fitzgerald, who happens to be the godmother of my youngest son, Damon, was among the first winners.

One group appearing on that night's show was the Imperials. A wonderful group out of Philadelphia, the Imperials had a recording called "To Those That Wait," which had become a favorite of our group. So we decided we would perform that song. We had the nerve to sing it while the Imperials stood in the wings listening to us. And guess what? We won the amateur hour. The Imperials were happy for us and told us we did a wonderful job.

The Apollo Theater stage became and remains the barometer by which many performers determine whether they'll succeed in this business. The saying goes, "If you can make it at the Apollo, you can make it anywhere."

That Wednesday evening was also the start of the Gospelaires' entry into the world of background singing in the recording studios of New York. A young man approached all the groups performing on this particular show and asked if they could do a background session at Savoy Records in Newark. So I spoke up and told the man that my group would do it. He said okay and asked us to meet him at the Savoy Records studios, where we did a session with Sam "the Man" Taylor, a big-toned saxophone player, and Nappy Brown, a popular R&B and blues singer.

As a result of that first date, the Gospelaires fast became the female voices of choice for background work in New York. We worked behind some of the biggest recording artists of that time: the Shirelles, Ray Charles, Dinah Washington, Ben E. King, Chuck Jackson, the Exciters, Tommy Hunt, Solomon Burke, and the Drifters, just to name a few.

So at age seventeen, while in my senior year preparing to graduate from East Orange High School, my career had begun. But all the studio work had to be scheduled for the weekends. Our parents were not going to allow anything to interfere with our schoolwork. On weekends, we hopped on the 118 bus that took us from Newark to the Port Authority Bus Terminal near Times Square in New York City. From there, we'd catch the subway to where the recording studios were located. We worked quickly and diligently to get our parts down on the first take, if possible, so we could rush back home to East Orange.

Eventually, graduation day came, and my entire summer was spent doing more studio work. I could certainly use the money, since I was entering the Hartt College of Music that September. I had a partial scholarship from my church, but the money I earned doing background sessions during the summer was a huge help in paying for tuition, books, rent, and food. I arranged my classes so that I could do studio work in New York Thursdays through Saturdays, and then be back in Hartford by Sunday to resume classes on Monday.

I became known as the "demo queen," and a young man named Jimmy Breedlove was known as the "demo king." Songwriters used demos, or demonstration recordings, to showcase their song for record executives. Back then, a demo was the key to whether a writer's song was chosen for release. I did demos for many songwriters and music publishers, particularly those who were in the Brill Building in Manhattan. I also remember spending hours at another building, on Seventh Avenue and Forty-seventh Street, where a recording studio called Associated was located. I would record one demo after another after another. This was an exciting time in my life.

DIONNE'S LESSONS LEARNED

- *Remove "can't" from your vocabulary. As Grandpa told me, "If you can think it, you can do it!"*

- *Establish a strong spiritual foundation. This will help sustain you through life's peaks and valleys.*

- *It's never too late to pursue a passion. Do what makes you happy.*

- *Encourage children to follow their dreams. Let them reach for the stars, and let them know you'll be there no matter what.*

- *Create a support mechanism. Family is extremely important.*

CHAPTER 2

Don't Make Me Over

D URING THE late 1950s and early 1960s, the Brill Building on Broadway was full of songwriters such as Carole King and Gerry Goffin, Jerry Leiber and Mike Stoller, Phil Spector, and Burt Bacharach and Hal David. In this fascinating place, these writers created the music that has become the sound track of all our lives. When you walked into the building, it felt like you'd just stepped onto hallowed ground. Jerry Leiber and Mike Stoller were recording the Drifters in the Atlantic Records studio when they called us, the Gospelaires, to do a session with them in July 1961. The song we were singing background for was "Mexican Divorce." Also in the Atlantic Records studio with us that day was Burt Bacharach, the session's arranger and conductor. He had cowritten "Mexican Divorce" with Bob Hilliard.

Burt approached me after the session and asked if I would be interested in singing on a few demos for him and a new writing partner of his, Hal David. I said, "Cool!" and soon I was in the studio recording demos for them.

The connection to Leiber and Stoller led to work with some of the brightest R&B acts of that time, such as the Exciters, Garnet Mimms, and Scepter Records recording artists Chuck Jackson, Tommy Hunt, Maxine Brown, and the Shirelles.

I was making enough money to buy my first car. My new used yellow sports car actually saved me money because I could now drive down to New York from Connecticut for less than it cost to take the train.

I was always conscious of money management, even early in my career. I guess that's something I picked up from my father. I worked hard for the money and was mindful not to waste it, even in the days when I didn't make much; and that has served me well throughout my career.

Back then, the Gospelaires' recording sessions pay rate was different from that of most background singers. The union scale for each background singer at that time was $22.50 for each side of the record she sang on or per hour, whichever was the greater. But since we were not in the union, I could charge whatever I wanted to, and I did. I charged $45.00 per side per singer or per hour, whichever was the greater. Also, being the contractor of the group, I was paid double.

One of the demos I recorded for Burt and Hal was "It's Love That Really Counts." Burt took the demo to Florence Greenberg, owner of Scepter Records, with the hope that she would use it for the Shirelles to record. Florence, as it turned out, was not interested in the song but rather in my voice. "Forget the song," she said. "Get the girl singer."

Florence was the only female at this time that I was aware of to own and operate a recording company. She used to say she was "a white woman in a black business who couldn't carry a tune." Florence came to the music business as a housewife and mom from Passaic, New Jersey. She had two children, Mary Jane and Stanley. But her roster of artists at Scepter also became her children and would include the Isley Brothers, the Shirelles, Chuck Jackson, Maxine Brown, Tommy Hunt, B. J. Thomas, Ronnie Milsap, Nick Ashford and Valerie Simpson, and eventually me. Against all odds, Florence was very successful and remained so until the large conglomerates such as Columbia Records and the WEA (Warner Elektra Atlantic) Corporation began to buy out the smaller labels such as Scepter.

Florence enjoyed music. Before she founded Scepter Records, Florence spent a lot of her free time at Hill and Range, a well-known music publishing company in New York. She placed songs for songwriters, mingled with performers and others in the music industry, and got to know about the business.

In 1958, with two associates, she started the Tiara label. Thanks to her teenage daughter, Mary Jane, who went to school with the Shirelles, Florence had heard about four girls at Passaic High School who sang like angels. Shirley Owens, Beverly Lee, Addie "Micki" Harris, and Doris Coley called themselves the Poquellos. Florence was eager to sign them. Remember, this was also around the time that "girl groups" like the Chantels were popular. The bad news was that the girls weren't interested. Florence pursued them for two years before they agreed to record. They had just written a song titled "I Met Him on a Sunday" that was just right for the label, too. The group got a record deal with Tiara and changed its name to the Shirelles. And sure enough, the single took off.

"I Met Him on a Sunday" reached number 49 on the *Billboard* chart in the spring of 1958. But the Shirelles' success turned out to be more than the tiny label could manage. Florence, a persistent promoter, was exhausted. She sold Tiara and the Shirelles' contract to the larger and better-established Decca label. Decca released two Shirelles singles, but when neither did well, Decca gave the group back to Florence, who decided to start yet another record label. This time she was better prepared; she had more experience, savvy, knowledge, and better connections. She called the new incarnation of her label Scepter.

Meanwhile, my demo-recording career with Burt and Hal was going well. One song that I thought was particularly wonderful was "Make It Easy on Yourself." I instantly fell in love with this song. As our work relationship continued, they started asking me if I would consider recording as a solo artist. It sounded exciting, but I knew that wasn't going to happen because my mother would not agree. She was adamant that her children's education should come first and be completed before any of us even thought about doing anything else.

Nonetheless, I told Burt and Hal that I would ask my family and get back to them, even though I already knew what Mommy's answer would be. But I asked anyway, and she answered no as expected. I then went to my dad. He, of course, asked if I had asked my mom, and when I answered that she had said no, he said, "I guess the answer then is no." I respected my parents and would never defy them, but I thought about it and came up with a plan. I asked Mommy if I could do it on the condition that I arranged to record on weekends only. She considered it and relented. I presented the conditions to Burt and Hal, and they both agreed. I also told them that "Make It Easy on Yourself," the song I had fallen in love with, had to be one of my first recordings. They agreed to this, too. So I signed a production agreement with Burt and Hal, and a recording contract with Florence. This began a long relationship with

Scepter Records and with Bacharach and David. They were elated. And I went back to Hartt very happy and excited.

Then one day soon after, I was driving home from Hartt when I heard the great Jerry Butler on the radio singing "Make It Easy on Yourself." I was truly upset with Burt and Hal and went to have a little talk with them. I reminded them of the promise they made to me. "We have a problem here. You want me to record with you? I am who I am. Don't make me over, man!" In other words, don't lie to me or tell me one thing and do something else.

I guess fate has a way of righting wrongs. The language I used to deploy my burst of anger and frustration gave Burt and Hal the inspiration to write what became my first recording with Scepter, "Don't Make Me Over," released in 1962.

But "Don't Make Me Over" almost didn't happen. In my first session, we had recorded only three songs: "Don't Make Me Over," "I Smiled Yesterday," and a third song; two of them would form the A and the B sides of my first release. Florence, being the emotional woman that she was, was in anguish because she hated both sides of the record, but with only three recordings to choose from, there was nothing else to do for the first release. "I Smiled Yesterday" was designated as the A side of the recording. But thanks to a radio disc jockey in Detroit named Ernie Durham, who flipped the recording and started playing the B side, "Don't Make Me Over" began to pick up in popularity. Although "I Smiled Yesterday" charted, "Don't Make Me Over" was the side people really wanted to hear, and in early 1963, it became my first Top 40 hit. As it is said, "All's well that ends well."

Another wrong that ultimately worked out had to do with a label misprint on "Don't Make Me Over." My surname *Warrick* was misspelled *Warwick* before anyone caught the mistake. By then the recording was well on its way up the record charts. I wanted to pull the record to have the spelling corrected but was promised that the correction would be made on the second pressing. Apparently, that never happened. I remained a *wick* instead of a *rick*. The Warwick name has served me well, and it did not seem to bother my parents or my grandparents very much, since they looked on it as a "professional" name. This made me feel a lot better about the mistake. Dee Dee, when she started recording, was lucky enough not to have had that mistake made on the labels of her records and maintained the name Warrick.

The more well known I became, the more people attempted to describe my vocal style. Some would say it was classical or pop. But gospel has been and always will be first and foremost in my world of music. The same is true of many others among the greatest voices. Many of us have come out of the church, like my dear friend Aretha Franklin. The comfort and joy associated with singing the songs that inspire and tell the lessons of the Bible cannot be beat. But I chose not to confine myself to singing religious music. There were whispers of criticism from within church circles about my decision to make recordings of popular music my profession. And that came as a surprise to me. I was a bit anxious about it, but my grandfather had my back. He stood in his pulpit one Sunday morning and acknowledged hearing some of the negative comments regarding me and my choice to sing "secular" music. He let all of those who had something to say know that his baby "Little D" was a child of God who had been given a special gift and was using this gift to inspire and lift people in the way God meant for her to do. He let all know that I was making an honest living and doing so with dignity. He then did something totally unexpected: he had the congregation stand and give me my second congregational standing ovation.

Criticism in general doesn't hurt me, particularly if it's constructive. But sometimes criticism can be delivered in a way intended to
destroy people, not help them become better. Fortunately, purely
destructive criticism has never gained the upper hand in my career.

Knowing and believing in the words and worth of prayer have
given me the strength to endure this. As my grandfather also said
to me: "Baby, you just let them run their mouths, and you run your
business." He reminded me that people spurned Jesus Christ, and
to say to myself in this situation *Who am I?* I am still living by those
words.

So I continued to "run my business," and good things continued
to happen for me. With my first royalty check from "Don't Make
Me Over," I did what most children would love to be able to do for
their parents: I asked my mommy and daddy to start house hunting,
and they did. They found a dream house in Orange, New Jersey,
and I got the pleasure of putting a smile on my parents' faces. As
my touring increased, so did my funds, allowing me to continue to
shower gifts on my parents and siblings.

This was a very exciting time for me. I also heard myself on the
radio for the first time. I was driving home from the airport and
heard "Don't Make Me Over" on Murray the K's radio show out of
New York. Murray "the K" Kaufman was one of the most popular
and powerful radio disc jockeys in the country.

I pulled over to the side of the road, turned the radio up as loud
as I could, and grinned until my cheeks hurt. It still excites me to
hear my recordings on radio, though it doesn't occur as often as it
did "back in the day."

BEING WITH Scepter gave me a solid foundation and knowledge
of the record industry. Burt, Hal, and I became known through-

out the industry as "the triangle marriage that worked." Hal David was, and still is, one of the most prolific poets I have had the pleasure to work with. He is thoughtful, gentle, sincere, and a wonderful human being—a reflection of the kind of lyrics he writes. He was the levelheaded one of the trio.

Burt was the handsome one, and extremely talented. I referred to him as "society's child" because his dad, Bert, was a recognized writer and columnist, and his mother, Irma, a wonderful woman, was very much a socialite. Burt's star was on the rise from having become music director for some of our well-known singers such as Merv Griffin, Vic Damone, and the legendary Marlene Dietrich. He set the bar high musically with his arrangements of lush strings and unusual time signature changes. His complex and powerful arrangements have put many musicians to the test.

My recording sessions at Scepter over seven years were always wonderful. I was always in the A studio, the largest one they had, with a full orchestra: horns, strings, rhythm section, percussion, sometimes a harp, and background chorus. Phil Ramone was the engineer behind the glass. Hal David would be in the studio, and once in a while my mom and, of course, Florence. The studio would be booked for a three-hour session, with a built-in half hour overtime, if needed.

The Gospelaires did the background vocals on all of my recordings and continued to do this when I left the group to go solo. Dee Dee took over my position as the contractor for the sessions, and Cissy became a member of the group. Working with family in my case was easy and loads of fun, and artistically it benefited us to have the blend of voices to create a "family" sound.

It's no wonder that I'm spoiled when it comes to recording. These days the recording process involves putting together tracks already done mostly by computers. Rarely are live musicians used, and all of the vocal parts are sung with the singer and the engineer the only ones in the studio. It's rather lonely and very different from how I used to record.

Another difference between then and now is the length of time it takes to record an "album." Then, we were able to do a complete album in a week's time, take another couple of weeks for mixing and mastering, and within a three- to four-week period, our product was in the marketplace. To block out a studio for an entire year was unheard of. But that seems to be common today. There is a tale of an artist, who will remain unnamed, going into the studio to do a project. All she would do is listen to tracks already recorded, sing maybe two or three notes, leave, and not go back into the studio for a couple of weeks, then return to put another two or three notes on what she had sung before. This would've driven me crazy.

"Don't Make Me Over" was a hit and turned out to be just the beginning of a wonderful relationship between Burt, Hal, and me. It was also the first indication that my style would appeal to a wide and diverse audience. I enjoyed enormous initial success with that song, which also started a four-year run of consecutive Hot 100 pop hit singles on the *Billboard* chart. I became the first African American female artist to achieve such an accomplishment. I had a total of thirty-two Hot 100 hits over the next seven years, fifteen of which were Top 30 and eight of which were Top 10.

I N 1963 I became one of Scepter's star acts and started touring.

Like most African American artists during that time, I experienced my very first solo performance on the road in the South— Atlanta, Georgia, to be exact. It was at the Royal Peacock, owned by Henry Wynn, an African American manager and promoter. The Royal Peacock was a legendary nightclub and "hot spot" of Atlanta.

The space held around three hundred people and had a nice dance floor where folks could let loose. For me, it was big deal to perform there because many of the biggest names in show business had done so, including James Brown, Little Richard, Otis Redding, Ike and Tina Turner, Jackie Wilson, and Sam Cooke.

My sister, Dee Dee, and Estelle Brown went along with me and sang background. But I gotta say that we were in no way prepared for the audience. This was a down-home blues and R&B club. It was the real Southern deal. And it was all new to me. The folks who frequented the Royal Peacock were not only used to amazing R&B entertainers, but also to great blues artists such as B.B. King, Bobby "Blue" Bland, and "Little" Esther Phillips. At this time, the early '60s, I was considered a pure pop artist. So I was breaking new ground, a rarity among African American singers.

The first night was by no means a great success. I was clearly in over my head. The folks were kind enough not to boo me. I received maybe one or two handclaps, if that. It was certainly not the Brooklyn Fox Theater in New York, where I had early on experienced a successful performance with audience participation. In Atlanta, it was almost as if they didn't know who I was, and it seemed that they really didn't care. Refusing to fail, I decided to try something on the second night that I had done at rehearsal with Dee Dee and Estelle. I did my records, all three of them—"Don't Make Me Over," "Walk On By," and "Anyone Who Had a Heart"—and then I told the band, such as it was, to start the vamp of a Ray Charles song, "What'd I Say."

Well, you would have thought "Ms. Pop Singer" walked off the stage and another artist had magically appeared, because the audience woke up and began singing with me. Some even got up and started dancing. This was also a new and exciting experience for me.

I was a hit. Mr. Wynn, the Royal Peacock owner, also operated a company called Super Sonic Attractions. He could pull together a tour of some of the best R&B talent in the country in those days. He asked me if I would like to do one of his tours, and, of course, I said yes. Soon after that, I was booked on my first tour, the Sam Cooke tour.

This performance at the Royal Peacock stands out because it was where I first bridged my live pop style with blues and R&B. For me as an artist, it was a rewarding experience. And as my recording career grew, I became known as the "artist who bridged the gap," meaning that my recordings never found resistance on pop radio stations, and R&B radio stations continued to play my records. So I kinda opened doors for other African American artists to "cross over."

This tour starred Sam Cooke, along with the Drifters, Johnny Thunder, the Crystals, Betty Wright, "Little" Esther Phillips, Solomon Burke, and me. The flashy "Gorgeous George," whose name is Theophilus Odell George, was the emcee, and the Upsetters were the band. And believe me, that is just what they were: upsetting. Reading music was not their strong suit—especially my music. I never once heard them play the time signature changes and melodic notes of my material during the entire tour. It was frustrating for me, but somehow I survived.

The Upsetters band was not the only group who struggled with Burt's arrangements. I remember when I made my third appearance at the Apollo Theater and was to perform "Anyone Who Had a Heart." Burt decided he was going to rehearse the Apollo band for me, and although the musicians were good, they were not the quality of session players he was accustomed to having. Their sight-reading skills were not as swift, and they had trouble, putting a few more gray hairs on Burt's head in the process. He finally gave up. So Charles "Honi" Coles, the famed tap dancer who had become the

Apollo's stage manager, and I continued to rehearse the band many hours after Burt left. Finally, we got them where they needed to be to perform the song properly.

All kinds of things happen to make the entertainment business not always work well or always be fun. For example, during the 1963 tour, we traveled on a bus that on many occasions required the guys get out and push it. At some point, we became surprised that we made any of the gigs at all. The routing of our travels wasn't always so well thought out, either. Our route could look like this: Atlanta to Dallas to Toronto to North Carolina. You get the picture? There were times when we would arrive at our destination with just enough time to throw soap and water in strategic places and get onstage to do the show—an experience, to say the least.

Traveling through the South was in and of itself an adventure. Having been raised in the North, I didn't know much about racial discrimination, but my trip south gave me a fast lesson. The practice of having "colored" restrooms or "colored" sides of drinking fountains was not something I was aware of growing up where I did.

I was on tour in South Carolina and went to the front of the coliseum to use the restroom when I first saw the sign "colored" restroom, next door to the "white" restroom. Then I noticed that the water fountain was marked the same. I decided I would wait to go to the restroom, since I only needed to wash my hands. Curious, I tested the drinking fountain to see if the water on the side marked "colored" would have a different flavor.

As I bent to drink out of the "colored" side, a white woman bent to drink out of the side marked "white." We actually bumped heads. I started laughing. The woman, however, only looked at me blankly. I decided to say something.

"I was told I am not supposed to speak to you since you are a white person, but I have to say this to you: you are drinking out of your side, and I am drinking out of my side, and there is one pipe bringing the water to both sides of the fountain, so we are actually drinking the same water." Let me tell you, that woman turned red, as she almost choked. That was when the realization of just how stupid segregation and discrimination were really hit me.

Our tour bus was parked at the stage of the coliseum right by a little restaurant called the Toddle House. Sam asked us to go and get all of us something to eat. La La Brooks, the lead singer of the Crystals, wrote down what everybody on the bus wanted, then we went into the restaurant to get the sandwiches. There happened to be only two other people in the restaurant, and they were sitting in a booth. So La La and I sat at the counter, where we noticed a handsome African American man was the cook.

Well, this white waitress came rushing over, ordering us to get up from the counter. We thought she had lost her mind and quickly stood up. She ordered us to go to an area off to the side. When we got to where she told us to go, we figured that this is where she took her breaks because there was an ashtray with cigarette butts, a half cup of coffee, and a couple of aprons hanging on the wall. With that, I asked, "Can we get a menu?" The waitress snapped, "You will just shut up and wait until I get to you."

Being all of twenty-three years old and not used to being yelled at—especially by someone like this woman—I responded, "Hell no, we won't wait, and you can take the menus and shove them as far up your butt as you can get them!" La La and I then left and got back on the bus.

Less than five minutes later, a sheriff's car came to a screeching halt at the front of the bus. An officer stepped onto the bus demanding to see the two "colored girls" who were just in the Toddle House. Sam Cooke said to the officer, "There are no 'girls' on this bus, just young ladies. And what do you want with them?"

The officer said that the two young ladies had insulted the wait-ress, and he wanted them to apologize to her. Sam laughingly but politely asked the officer to leave the bus, since it was private prop-erty and he had not been invited on. The unspoken message was that no one on this bus would be giving an apology to anyone. The officer left in a huff. Sam said to La La and me, "I should have let him have you two. Just think of all the publicity we would have got-ten for this tour." The bus rocked with laughter.

Sam Cooke was a real cutie. He was a kind, gentle, and caring man who always had something nice to say to and about people. When I learned that Sam was having a party in his hotel suite one evening, I knocked on his door. When he saw it was me, he said, "I know your mother, and you can't come in here." He then walked me back to my room. I was upset at being excluded, but I knew that Sam meant well; he was very protective of me, like a father. I first met him on the gospel circuit while he was with the Soul Stirrers, whom the Drinkards would occasionally tour with. I loved being around him because he always had a smile on his face and was always humming either one of the gospel songs he used to sing or someone else's song that he loved.

The recordings of Sam's that were hits for him and made him famous are still favorites of mine. My eldest son, David, who played the part of Sam Cooke in the film *Ali*, has said many times that he would love to do a tribute in the form of a recording to Sam Cooke. And I think he should.

Songs such as "You Send Me," "Bring It On Home to Me," "A Change Is Gonna Come," to name a few, inspired many sing-along moments from the audience during the tour. And, well, the ladies just either sat with these strange smiles on their faces or made com-ments like "And you send me, too!" or "I'll bring it on home to you anytime!"

Sam was also a smart man who saw the importance of owning his songs. He took steps to copyright and publish them himself and owned his catalog—an unusual thing for an artist during this time in the music industry. Most would sell their writing rights to a publishing company.

The news of his death on December 11, 1964, a day before my twenty-fourth birthday, was devastating. I was going to Los Angeles for the first time, at his expense, to celebrate my birthday with him and some friends.

M Y NEXT Henry Wynn tour was with Jackie Wilson headlining, Chuck Jackson, the Orlons, and again Gorgeous George as emcee, and, yes, the Upsetters band. This tour, I remember, was a bit crazy because Jackie had no real concept of time—meaning he would show up whenever he wanted to regardless of when the show was supposed to start.

One time he decided not to show up at all. Gorgeous George was told to stand in front of a closed curtain and keep the audience entertained while, behind the curtain, the band loaded its instruments onto the bus to make a quick exit. But the audience became suspicious and stormed the stage to find that we were all on the bus ready to leave. This was scary, as the crowd began to rock the bus and nearly turned it over. We were lucky to get out of there with our lives.

Progress isn't always improvement, at least not for artists on the road. This same tour happened as some racial discrimination was ending. We were able, for the first time, to stay at a Sheraton Hotel. My standard room was fine, but Jackie and Chuck weren't so lucky with their suites. We found that out when we heard screaming come from their floor. Jackie, a former Golden Gloves boxer, was in the hall fighting bats—yes, the flying kind. I couldn't believe my eyes. There he was boxing bats with his bare hands, throwing jabs and hooks, and shuffling his feet as if he were in some kind of championship boxing match. And then he threw his hands up in the air as if he'd won the match. I said to myself, This man is crazy. There were bats in Chuck's suite as well. It took me all of ten minutes to get my bags and me out of that hotel. I checked into the Holiday Inn three blocks away.

Jackie Wilson was another man who impressed me. He was very handsome, and because he had been a boxer, he had great moves that were quite evident when he performed. Women loved him, and he loved women. In 1975 he suffered a stroke onstage while performing "Lonely Teardrops" during a Dick Clark show at the Latin Casino in Camden, New Jersey, and fell into a coma. He died in 1984 at the age of forty-nine.

Both Sam and Jackie made their transitions much too soon; Sam was only thirty-three when he was shot to death in Los Angeles. I truly miss both of them.

TOURING WAS hard work, but also very exciting. We didn't make much money back then, but that wasn't our motivation for doing what we did. We loved the music most of all. Don't get me wrong: we did want to get paid, and sometimes it was hard to collect, despite the fact that we'd earned it.

In fact, getting paid fairly for my performances seemed to be more work than the show itself. There was a term used to describe the contracts we signed back then: "slave contracts."

All recording artists, especially those who were considered R&B artists, tended to sign contracts blindly, and I was no different. We often did not realize that we were charged for recording costs: studio time, musicians, engineers, assistant engineers, music arrangements (most of which we never received), background singers, and the list goes on.

Back then, the record companies would pay us a royalty rate of 2½ percent of 90 percent of the money earned from the sales of records, less what was called "breakage" and "free goods" (records given away for free to disc jockeys, writers, and others who might promote it). By the time this math was done, the artist's share was brought down to a mere pittance. Pretty slick, eh?

For example, let's say a record earned $1. The artist got 2½ percent of 90 cents, or roughly 2 cents per record, before the breakage and other costs were thrown in. We were given raises in royalty payments up to 6 percent, but none of the tacked-on costs ever decreased. So in essence, the royalty rate raise, when we got it, actually meant nothing.

We were young, naïve, and just wanted to make music and enjoy our newfound fame. Thank goodness, I had a father who raised questions on my behalf. He reviewed one of my royalty statements and discovered that I was being shortchanged. It wasn't only in the terms of the deal, either. Just imagine having an attorney representing you, and that same attorney representing the record company and one of the producers. Obviously, this is not a fair situation, and yet it was common throughout the industry. And yes, that happened to me. It doesn't take an expert to see a conflict of interest in this scenario. I still wonder why record companies, already having a contractual advantage, felt the need to exploit us further through these cozy backroom relationships.

I wonder if there ever was an actual true accounting of the records I sold by *any* record company I worked with back in the '60s or, sadly, to this very day. I wonder what difference it would have made if I had been given a true accounting of my record sales back then. I think I would have been a very wealthy young lady, at the very least.

Let's look at the heights I reached early in my career during the years 1964 through 1971. (Of course, these numbers would not include my worldwide record sales through the entire '70s, '80s, '90s, and right up to the present date.) It was reported that I sold well over 35 million recordings, 16 million in the United States alone. Even at the lowly 3 cents royalty, which was later bumped to 6 cents, I'd have been a happy camper. *Cash Box* magazine, a prominent recording industry publication that recognized the best-selling artists, presented me with honors in 1964, 1966, 1967, 1968, 1969, 1970, and 1971 for being a Best Selling Artist. Isn't that a reason to wonder whether fair accounting procedures were followed? At best, accounting records regarding artist royalties were very poorly or very creatively kept. Makes you want to go "hmm." Even my own audits of Scepter Records showed that the label kept bad accounting records.

In those days, everybody was being robbed by their record companies. I can only imagine the deals less successful artists received. I had what I thought was leverage in negotiating my deals because I was considered a major recording artist.

My crossover appeal was one of the factors in my success. My music was played on African American radio stations as well as white radio stations. Most of the African American jocks knew I was African American because they had presented shows that I appeared on at the Apollo, the Uptown Theater in Philadelphia, the Regal Theater in Chicago, the Howard Theater in Washington, DC, and all of the other theaters that were usually included on tours that covered what was then called "the chitlin' circuit." White radio didn't always know what nationality I was.

But I also did what were called the "premium" tours with most of the white pop acts of the time. These tours were presented by Dick Clark, Irving Feld, and Murray the K, and included acts such as the Four Seasons, Jay and the Americans, Bobby Rydell, Chubby Checker, the Orlons, Little Eva, the Shirelles, and me, just to name a few. These premium tours paid a little more money than the chitlin' circuit, and the accommodations were better. And the bus actually ran properly. We were being thrust in front of what were predominantly white audiences, and as an artist, I was able to build a loyal following of fans.

These tours also helped open some other doors for me—like my appearance on Dick Clark's *American Bandstand* show in 1963. This was one of the very first national television shows I did. My appearance also let everybody across America know that I was African American. Dick Clark always made me feel comfortable. He was and is to this very day easy to be around. I remember this appearance as if it were yesterday. The record I was promoting at that time was "Don't Make Me Over," and I was very excited. It was much like when I played the Apollo for the first time. The saying is "If you make it on *Bandstand*, you've got it made." I don't know who coined that phrase, but it did ring true. That is because *Bandstand* was one of the most highly rated TV shows, and millions of record-buying kids watched it religiously. Before fall 1963, the show aired every weekday afternoon, and then it switched to once a week, on Saturdays. Everyone who was anyone appeared on *Bandstand*, and that appearance practically ensured record sales.

After I sang, Dick came over to do a little interview with me. He noticed that I had my hand behind my back. He whispered, "Why do you have your hand behind your back?" And I whispered back to him, "The zipper in my dress broke while I was performing!" Dick, being the gracious and, thank God, quick-thinking man he is, reached around my waist and grasped the area of the dress that I had been holding. This allowed me to put my arm down by my side and not look awkward while doing the interview. So, I guess you could say I had the first near wardrobe malfunction. Ironically, my crossover success in pop prompted something that came as a big surprise: the decline of airplay for my records on African American radio. In fact, when I asked one of New York's premier jocks, Rocky G (the "G" stood for Grosse), program director for WWRL, why he was not playing my records on his show, he told me I was "too white."

When my recording of "Alfie" became number one on Rocky G's playlist in the summer of 1967, I called his show one evening while he was playing the song and anonymously asked, "Why are you playing that white girl's record?" He angrily answered, "That is no white girl, and who is this?" I started laughing and said, "This is the one you told was too white to play on your show. This is Dionne." We laughed about that for many years after.

Excited by the success of "Don't Make Me Over," Scepter quickly released two other singles, "This Empty Place," and another that made the R&B charts, "Make the Music Play." But it would be my next single, "Anyone Who Had a Heart," that became a hit and surpassed "Don't Make Me Over" in popularity and sales. It reached number 8 on the pop charts in early 1964. "Anyone Who Had a Heart" was also a hit in the United Kingdom, but it was not my recording. Through the years, the British have played a major role in the success of many Africian American artists, including mine.

THINGS STARTED picking up with my personal appearances. I started making a bit more money, and that afforded me the opportunity to do some more things for my family. My old sports car, which I had purchased used, had served me well all during my college years, but now I could afford to buy myself a brand-new yellow Mustang convertible.

The recordings, personal appearances, and growing popularity were wonderful, but the most exciting thing that happened to me was an appearance on *The Ed Sullivan Show.*

Everybody knew that a request to do the Sullivan show, which aired on Sunday nights from 1948 to 1971, in and of itself equaled success. It was the most important television show on the air, and it could bring an artist immense exposure—after all, about 35 million people watched the show every week. Mr. Sullivan's variety show introduced mainstream America to many who became the biggest artists of their time. The Beatles, the comedian George Carlin, and the Italian mouse puppet Topo Gigio were mixed in with Mr. Sullivan's taste for classical music and ballet, with artists like pianist Van Cliburn, opera singer Roberta Peters, and ballet dancer Rudolf Nureyev.

He took a special interest in African American performers. Given the times and the millions of people who watched his show, his willingness to book African American artists was an enormous help in breaking down the walls of segregation. America got to see gifted talents such as Nat "King" Cole, James Brown, Leontyne Price, Ella Fitzgerald, Mahalia Jackson, Richard Pryor, and many others. I appeared on his wonderful show five times.

I remember every one of those appearances, but what I remember most was that Mr. Sullivan could never pronounce my name correctly. I was "Diane," or "Danna," or "Dayonne," until a producer came up with the bright idea to spell my name phonetically as "D—ON" on Mr. Sullivan's cue card. From that time forward, he pronounced my name properly.

I also remember the kind way he treated me. He would ask me questions and give little tidbits of information about me to his audience. This was something I never saw him do with other acts that performed on his show. I later was told that he thought I was "special." This made me feel and know that, *yes,* I had truly arrived.

Because of my relationship with Burt and Hal early in my career, I met many other interesting people who also made me feel I had arrived. Once in a while, some of these introductions blossomed into true friendships.

While heading into their office in the Brill Building for rehearsal one day, I crossed paths with Marlene Dietrich. I couldn't believe my eyes at first. Flustered, I asked both Burt and Hal if they saw her. They smiled at my excitement and then explained that Burt was her musical director and was getting ready to go on tour with her. She had come to rehearse as well. I was truly impressed. She was a true international star of the era, having enjoyed success on screen in both silent and "talkie" movies, on stage, and as a recording artist.

My second meeting with Marlene occurred around 1964, when I was invited to appear a second time at the Olympia Theatre in Paris. Burt had called her to let her know that I was coming and asked her to take care of me while I was there.

She met me on the airport tarmac, and we were driven in a limousine to my hotel, where she had already checked me in. We went from the hotel to the Olympia, where she proceeded to do my stage lighting. Afterward, she asked to see my wardrobe. I took her to my dressing room to show her my clothes. She looked at each of my dresses, turned up her nose, and threw each of them into the hall. I thought she had lost her mind. I picked up the dresses and brought them all back into my dressing room. I was getting a bit upset and asked her what her problem was. Marlene looked at me and, in that deep German accent (I can still hear her voice in my head) said, "You cannot wear those things. They are not couture, and you must wear only couture."

And with that, she took me to Fashion Row, where I was introduced to the likes of Balmain, Saint Laurent, and Chanel. I became very familiar with couture and high fashion, much to the chagrin of my accountants. I will never forget that opening night at the Olympia. It was also my birthday, and a large box came for me at the theater. Inside was a gold Balmain gown, a gift from Marlene Dietrich. I appear in the gown on the cover of my album *Here I Am.* Since I was basically on my own in Paris, this attention was quite welcome. It was a comfort to know she had my back. I learned so much from her and started referring to her as "Momma," and she seemed to like that. Mostly, she taught me about dressing properly. For example: "When you wear a gown," she explained, "it is not considered one unless it either touches the floor or the tip of the toe of your shoe." I have never forgotten that, and it is a rule of thumb for those of us who are required to wear gowns.

She helped me to refine my image, and I saw the result of that because I became known for how I presented myself on and off stage. I received many comments from fans, and ladies both young and old tried to imitate this elegant image.

Marlene Dietrich helped, but my introduction to style and image started with the ladies in my family: my mother and her sisters. They were very stylish in their choices of clothing, and their "crowning glory," their hair, which was always in style and in place. Clifford Peterson was the professional who took care of my hair and created what fast became known as the "Dionne" cut. Many ladies let me know they were driving their hairdressers crazy trying to duplicate the look.

I was also influenced by Lena Horne, Diahann Carroll, and Loretta Young. Michael Travis was also very important; he created the "Dionne" look in terms of my stage wear. I would hear from many people that they couldn't wait to see what I was going to wear in my personal appearances. (I'll talk more about Clifford, Michael, and my image later.)

I have to say that some of what I see our young ladies wearing onstage today leaves me speechless—and not in a good way. Some of the clothes are just too revealing and lack class. However, I'm happy to see that some of the young artists who used to make me cringe are growing and learning how to present themselves more elegantly and work with our great designers of today. My image is one reason why I have enjoyed success and longevity in the entertainment business. However, it's the songs I have recorded over my

Lena Horne and me at Lena's award party.
(Personal collection of Dionne Warwick)

career that have made me known throughout the world. I've been blessed to have fifty-six charted hits, second only to my dear friend Aretha Franklin. And some of the songs from early in my career have interesting little stories behind them.

Prior to my recording "Message to Michael," it had two other titles. "Kentucky Bluebird" was the first title, and it was written for and recorded by Lou Johnson in 1964. It was a wonderful recording but did not appeal to radio and never gained attention in the market. "Message to Martha" was the song's second title and was sung by Jerry Butler. His version met the same resistance from radio that Lou's had. I recorded the song and used the name Michael in place of Martha to help Sacha Distel, a French composer, singer, and guitarist with whom I was working at the Olympia Theatre in Paris in 1966. He wanted to record the song in English to give to Florence with the hope that she would have him join the Scepter roster. Florence was at the session and told me this was my hit. She also said that she was not really looking to add to the Scepter family. This news disappointed Sacha, but then he graciously allowed my version using his arrangement to be used as my single. Every time he heard the song, he said, he took comfort in the fact that "At least I can sing in the same key as you."

"Wishin' and Hopin' " was never intended to be a single for me. It was to be a B side or an album cut. Dusty Springfield, a British pop singer, wanted to record this song. She was brought to the States to be produced by Burt and Hal. Because the song originally was written for me and first recorded by me, there was unfortunately no way to alter the musical arrangement, making Dusty's recording sound as if she used my track. Consequently, DJs and others said she had copied my version, right down to the breaths I took. I must say in her defense that she really had no choice; that was the way the song was structured. Dusty became a friend over the years and was a really talented singer. I miss her music, and I know the industry does, too.

Sometimes there are good reasons why a recording of the same song by different artists is an honest coincidence; other times there's something a bit sinister about the way it's done. "Anyone Who Had a Heart," for example, was just flat-out copied—note for note, word for word, and not very well, I might add—by the white British pop singer Cilla Black (whose real name is Cilla White; go figure). This upset me simply because "Anyone Who Had a Heart" had just been released in the States at the time. I introduced the song in Paris at the Olympia Theatre. I was to go to London to promote the record after I closed at the Olympia, and to my great surprise heard her recording when I arrived. Yes, I was p—— off and made it known. Yes, I met her, and we were somewhat cordial to each other. And no, I never got over it.

Because it was a well-known fact around this time that Burt and Hal wrote for me all of the songs I recorded, whenever someone else was heard singing one of their songs, it was thought that I had recorded it first. Such was the case with "What the World Needs Now Is Love." I was asked to consider recording the song, but the form it was in when I first heard it was better suited for a country singer, so I turned it down. Because Burt and Hal had promised to produce a record for Jackie DeShannon, they gave her the song and gave it the BDW—Bacharach, David, Warwick—formula: an arrangement and use of background vocals in a style usually associated with my recordings. It sounded as if I could have recorded it first, but, alas, it was Jackie who did.

A little-known fact is that my sister, Dee Dee, recorded "Alfie" before I did, and she did a wonderful rendition of it, too. As far as I am concerned, she should have had a hit with it, but the record was not aggressively promoted and didn't do as well as it could have.

"Alfie" had been recorded forty-two times before I did it, and I did it only because we needed another song to complete an album. To be honest, I did not want to record the song. With so many versions, what would be the point? As fate would have it, I was the only one to have a hit with it. Maybe 43 is a lucky number for me.

Tommy Hunt, who was a label mate at Scepter, was the first to record "I Just Don't Know What to Do with Myself" on one of his albums. It's a great recording. I recorded it long after he did. The only one other than me to have a hit record with this song was Dusty Springfield.

"I Say a Little Prayer" was written during the Vietnam War and seemed to resonate with listeners touched by the war. General Colin Powell and many others who fought in Vietnam have thanked me for "I Say a Little Prayer," letting me know how it got them through many difficult times. In 1997 the song was used in the film *My Best Friend's Wedding*. It was especially fun for me to watch the cast of characters having such a good time while singing the song. I also like the way the song was done by "Queen" Aretha, who made it her own.

People are often surprised to hear that I didn't accept every song Burt and Hal wrote for me to record. "Do You Know the Way to San Jose" was one such song. I hated it. I just could not believe Hal could or would ever write a lyric "whoa, whoa, whoa" and expect me to sing it. But I recorded it because of Hal. The song—and San Jose—meant something to him. And I cried all the way to the bank. I soon realized that I didn't know all the criteria needed to choose a hit.

"Promises, Promises" becoming a hit was a surprise to me, too. After all, it came from a Broadway show and is not a song you can dance to—which made its success even more curious. But people loved it. I'd even hear such unlikely folk as truck drivers humming it. The song is one of the most challenging of the Bacharach and

David compositions. Burt became known for creating compositions of this ilk, such as "Anyone Who Had a Heart." The time signature changes in "Promises, Promises" were enough to give most musicians a huge headache and proved to be a very daunting experience for the Broadway show's cast.

I have been asked by many of my peers, "How do you sing that stuff?" When presented with Burt's music, I did feel sometimes as if I were taking an exam. But, since he wrote the songs for me, I felt I was meant to be able to sing it. People have at times assumed that I wrote or cowrote many of the songs that I have been singing for years. Well, I certainly wish I had. I was the interpreter of songs written by Bacharach and David, as well as other composers. To me, those who have that ability to put words and music together, giving pleasure to the listening ear, have a very special talent. Also, those who are able to sing and record their works have an even more special talent.

I have written "a" song—not the most memorable of all that I have recorded. The song is titled "Two Ships Passing in the Night." If you remember it at all, I thank you. And for those who may never have paid the slightest bit of attention to it, well, it's okay, because you are in the majority!

Another wonderful song from the show *Promises, Promises* that I recorded was "I'll Never Fall in Love Again." I happened to be at the preview of the show in Boston when the decision was made to add it. Burt and Hal wrote the song in one day, and Jill O'Hara, who played the young love interest in the show, sang it sitting on the edge of the stage with guitar only. It became one of the highlights of the show. The great Ella Fitzgerald recorded it, but radio did not give it the airplay it deserved. I was getting ready to go back into the studio to record at the time, and Burt and Hal thought I should record the song. I thought they had lost it, thinking that I was going to cover an Ella Fitzgerald recording. Not! It was well after her recording proved not to be the hit it should have been that I recorded the song. My rendition, to my good fortune, was a hit. I am proud to say that Ms. Fitzgerald graciously thanked and congratulated me by telegram for my success with the song. "I'll Never Fall in Love Again" also earned me a Grammy Award.

"This Girl's in Love with You" was an album cut for me, but it was written at the request of trumpeter and bandleader Herb Alpert. He asked Burt (who at the time was on Herb's label, A&M Records) if he and Hal could write a song for his TV special. It was the kind of song that I think any recording artist would have loved to sing and record, and many artists have done so over the years.

If I had to choose a favorite Burt and Hal song, it would be "The Windows of the World." Hal's lyric for the song is pure poetry. The message of its words probably rings with greater truth now than when he wrote them in the 1960s. "The Windows of the World" became my mild "protest" song that talked about the problems of the world and the solutions.

"Walk On By" was another of those recordings that got popular because of a DJ. Murray the K of WINS in New York made it a contest song. He asked listeners to choose the side they liked best, and "Walk On By" won hands down.

Isaac Hayes's version of "Walk On By" was incredible. Nothing about his delivery of it resembled mine. It's sexy and soulful. The sensuality he brought to his version took the meaning of "Walk On By" to another level.

Isaac was like a big brother to me, and he sometimes got on my nerves being big brother. I met him shortly after he recorded "Walk On By" around 1969. I told him that I thought his version was, in my opinion, the definitive cover version of the song. He informed me that there were a few other songs that I had recorded that he intended to cover, and I let him know I would be eager to hear how he would treat them.

In the mid-'70s, the suggestion to go on tour with him was brought to me. It sounded interesting, since it was so unusual. Just picture: Isaac Hayes—chains, tights, bare chested; me—designer gowns, sophisticated, and very "girly." Most definitely the Odd Couple. Once we decided that we would do the tour, I had to let him know that he would have to revamp his wardrobe. Tuxedos would have to be his attire, as I had no intention of sharing a stage with him wearing his current outfit. He made this concession, and the show "A Man and a Woman" was born. It was received enthusiastically as we toured worldwide off and on for five years. We also set attendance records at most of the places we performed.

At a show in Sydney, Australia, Isaac gave me one of my most prized birthday gifts. It was a beautiful melody that was later given wonderful words by Adrienne Anderson. That song was "Déjà Vu," which Isaac wrote while recuperating from a water skiing accident. I cherish this gift and will always pay homage to him when I sing it.

Most people thought that he and I had a thing going on, and I guess if I had been sitting in the audience at any of our shows, I would have thought so, too. We loved to flirt with each other. However, I was newly divorced at that time, and the last thing I wanted was another relationship.

In 2008 Isaac and I were both looking forward to performing "Walk On By" onstage together once again at an event in Delaware. Sadly, he made his transition two months before our scheduled appearance. I miss my brother. However, he remains in my heart, and I am thankful that I had the opportunity to know him and can still enjoy his music.

In 1981 Luther Vandross released the definitive version of "A House Is Not a Home." Luther called me to let me hear it before it was released. The song was so beautifully done, I was at a loss for words.

When the NAACP honored me in December 1986 as entertainer of the year at the Image Awards, Luther was my surprise of the evening. He gave an ultimate performance of "A House Is Not a Home," singing directly to me. He brought me to tears. I told him after the show that he really did not have to show off that much, but I was happy that he did.

Luther will always hold a special place in my heart. I met him in the late '70s while I was performing at Carnegie Hall in New York. My aunt Cissy had just finished doing a session with him and brought him to the theater to meet me. He told me how much he loved my music and me and then proceeded to tell me the story of how he would tell people he was related to me. He said that he was found out when I was to appear in Michigan where he was studying, and his roommate asked if he was going to see his "cousin." Luther told me, "I just started sweating and said I had a terrible stomachache and would not be going to the show." He later confessed to his roommate that he was not related to me. We laughed about this and became great friends. As a matter of fact, I would sometimes tell people myself that we were related, which pleased him very much.

His untimely transition in 2005 at the age of fifty-four hurt me, as I am certain it did so many others. It was as if I'd lost a family member. I read the eulogy at his funeral, which was attended by so many of his friends and fans. I miss him very much. We talked to each other practically every day.

E VERY TIME it rained on the nights we were in the studio recording in New York, the record we cut became a hit. So rain and a certain Chinese restaurant called the China Song became part of a ritual we established in our work. If it rained, we went to the China Song after recording to have something to eat or a drink. We spent a lot of time at the China Song.

Things got rough, however, when we had to follow the music industry to California in the late '60s, where it hardly ever rains and there was no China Song. We lost our luck with making hits. However, it rained like crazy the night I recorded "Then Came You" with the Spinners in 1974. The Spinners complained about the weather, but all I could do was smile.

DIONNE'S LESSONS LEARNED

- *Success is unpredictable, so remember that patience truly is a virtue.*

- *Always have a backup plan.*

- *Hold your ground; don't compromise.*

- *Establish a mentor relationship with someone experienced in the area you are interested in pursuing.*

- *Learn to distinguish constructive criticism from destructive criticism; be receptive to constructive criticism, as it may be helpful to your career.*

CHAPTER 3

Do You Know the Way to San Jose

B ECOMING AN entertainer in the 1960s was quite interesting. It was a time of life-changing, history-making events that made the early days of my life in entertainment all the more intriguing. Racial discrimination was abounding, especially in the southern regions of our country; it was awful and in full swing. The civil rights movement, with its organized protests and marches, was bringing attention to the need for social and political change. By the end of the decade, people had had enough of the Vietnam War. Peace rallies became the rage, and "flower power" was the mantra of the hippie culture that emerged across the nation. Something called "free love" was a catchphrase of a generation, and was being openly practiced. They embraced the birth control pill and rebelled against the traditional roles society had assigned to men and women.

In the early '60s, I was sort of insulated and removed from much of what was going on. I was still a student at Hartt College, and though aware of the protests that were happening, I never took part in a march or rally. I wasn't completely out of touch, though. I was aware of a certain young senator named John F. Kennedy who was getting everyone's attention. I was impressed with his vision of a United States of America that allowed all citizens to prosper equally. He expressed his beliefs without fear, and his passion for his message spread throughout the country like wildfire.

Years later, I had the privilege of getting to know the family of that young senator through his sister-in-law Ethel. She was a fan of my music and would come to my shows, and as time went on, she became a friend. When I would perform at a venue called the Cape Cod Melody Tent in Hyannis, Massachusetts, she would come, bringing friends and family to the shows. She invited my sons to spend time at the Kennedy compound in Hyannis Port with the Kennedy children.

I also got to know Teddy Kennedy, the man who years later would be known as the "Lion of the Senate." He became a dear friend and my total champion, standing by me in my efforts to raise awareness of HIV/AIDS and other health-related issues. He brought to the Senate floor proposed legislation related to these topics and succeeded in getting important laws passed. I, like so many others, miss this wonderful man who fought so hard for those in need.

I MET MARTIN Luther King Jr. in the '60s through Aretha Franklin, who is his goddaughter. And though it was a brief meeting, it left a lasting impression on me. Although not a tall man in stature, he was a giant resonating power to me in the manner in which he spoke. His complete integrity of purpose was demonstrated by his tenacity, his belief in God Almighty, and his goal of peace and harmony for mankind.

I was preparing to go to Europe on tour and was watching television when President Kennedy was shot in 1963. Like everybody else, I could not believe what I was witnessing; time seemed to stop at that moment. I'll never forget it. Then, five years later, we lost the man named Martin. I was on an airplane heading to Kentucky to do a concert. The flight was a very rocky one because of a storm, and I was running very late. Neil Sedaka, who was appearing with me, and who had to extend his time onstage had sung all of his songs and then some, met me at the stage door entrance to tell me that Dr. King had been fatally shot. I still can't find the words to express how I felt. Two months later, Robert F. Kennedy was also assassinated. Malcolm X was another important leader we lost in that era, in early 1965. I learned about Malcolm X around the time I met Dr. King, but, unfortunately, much of what I heard about him was filtered through the news media that portrayed him as a radical, militant Muslim. He was judged unfairly, in my opinion. Religious beliefs are a personal choice that everyone should feel free to make without fear of ill treatment. Am I to be judged because I chose to accept Baptist beliefs and teachings? Are the Jews to be judged? Are the Hindus to be judged? Are the Christians to be judged because of their choice of religious beliefs? It is so easy to be and let be— why can't we just do that?

These assassinations left me, at a very young age, devastated, as they did the entire world. The assassinations of leaders who gave voice to people who had been so long ignored gave rise to organizations and leaders who took a more radical approach than King and the Kennedys did, such as the Black Panther Party. Being from the East Coast, I didn't know much about them. Like so many others, I was brainwashed into believing their only purpose was to encourage angry mobs. I now understand that they were wrongly depicted.

This was in fact an organization that included many highly educated people, prolific speakers, advocates for equal rights, and the list goes on. I began to take a closer look at what was happening around me.

ANOTHER MAN whom I have always greatly admired is "the Greatest," Muhammad Ali. He was known as Cassius Clay when I first met him at the Apollo Theater, where he had come to visit Chuck Jackson. We were impressed that Chuck knew him, but more impressed that he took the time to come to see our show. I'm not really a boxing fan, but he had a great presence (and good looks!). I've had the pleasure of being in his company several times since then and have made myself available whenever I could to perform at his fund-raising events. In 2008 I performed at celebrity fight night, his charity event, in Arizona.

Ali created enormous fear in the boxing ring, but when I was around him, he displayed enormous kindness. Everyone appreciated him and had no problem doing whatever could be done if he asked.

During the 1960s, I was trying to make a name for myself as a singer. "Don't Make Me Over" had made the charts, but I felt I had a ways to go. My recordings were being played all over Europe, though, and that was a pleasant surprise. I was invited by an impresario named Johnny Stark to go to France to do my first tour in Europe.

I performed on a British show very much like our *American Bandstand* called *Ready Steady Go!* and did record promotions for "Walk On By." I met Dusty Springfield, Engelbert Humperdinck, and many other UK entertainers on this trip. It was an amazing experience and gave me the opportunity to see places that I had only read about in my history books, as well as meet fellow artists.

I also appeared in Paris and performed on a show called "Les idoles des jeunes" (Idols of the Young) at the Olympia Theatre. The lineup included acts from Italy, Spain, and Belgium. The Shirelles, "Little" Stevie Wonder, and I were the American acts on the show. The prospect of appearing before a French audience was going to be interesting, given that they didn't really know what I looked like. Why? Because the albums of mine distributed in their market featured a photo of a white person on the cover. I didn't realize this until someone gave me an EP (extended-play recording, which usually contains about four songs) of mine that had on it a photo of someone else. It was quite a surprise.

Unfortunately, during this period, many record companies would market records by African American artists by not putting a photograph of the artists on the record cover. Instead they would put an image of a white person on the cover. It was wrongly assumed that white listeners would not purchase an album with an African American face on it.

Record companies weren't the only ones who got caught up in an artist's looks. I once had a red dress that I loved to wear onstage, but some of my fellow artists did not agree. The Shirelles, for some reason, hated that dress. I don't know why. They tried to get me not to wear it. Of course, I ignored them.

One night before the show, I put on the dress and joined everyone backstage at the bar area. Little Stevie came to me and said, "Dionne, you know I love you, don't you?"

"Yes I do," I replied, "and I love you, too." Then he said that he didn't want me to wear the red dress that I had on again because he thought "it was not the prettiest of the dresses" that I had been wearing.

I was surprised and actually shocked because I thought, *He can see!* Well, I rushed back to my dressing room, changed the dress, and never wore it again—only to find out later that the Shirelles had put Stevie up to it. Throughout the remaining shows, it eventually became obvious, as the Shirelles would stand outside my dressing room before each show, laughing while waiting to see what dress I wore. To this day, I don't know what happened to that red dress. But the thought of it still makes me smile.

Paris was wonderful, full of excitement and people one would see only in the movies. We were out almost every night at a discotheque called the St. Hilaire, where we saw people like Catherine Deneuve, Charles Aznavour, Michel Legrand, Johnny Hallyday, and so many others. The very handsome Anthony Quinn taught me to do a Greek dance.

I loved France and Europe. This was a change for me, as I soon realized that change is caused by circumstances. My lifestyle seemed to change overnight, for the better. It was a long way, in a short period of time, from my days on the chitlin' circuit. I had now experienced a taste of "the good life," and there would be no turning back.

Meeting Johnny Stark was in part responsible for that change. He spoiled me rotten, making sure that I traveled first class, stayed in five-star hotels, ate in the finest restaurants, and rode in limousines. He also introduced me to champagne, and not just any champagne. It was Cristal, and it's the only champagne I will drink. Early on, Johnny told me to accept nothing but what he was introducing me to—the best. And to this very day, those I work with—agents, my manager, business associates, my office staff—all feel this is the way I should be treated, and they make sure that "nothing but the best" is afforded me. And I'm grateful.

During the '60s, I was invited back several times to perform at the Olympia. My popularity grew so much I was even given a nickname, "the Black Orchid," and I loved it. Around this time, I also made my first trip to Brazil. I was booked to tour São Paulo, Brasília, and Rio. I was immediately smitten; my infatuation with Brazil would continue to grow over the years.

There is a long history of African American artists who become more successful or become successful more quickly abroad than in the United States. It's ironic and remains a mystery to me. My experience was the same in that my popularity was first realized in England and Paris, and later spread throughout the world. I performed before kings, queens, princes, princesses, and other royalty before ever being invited to perform at the White House. I had sold-out audiences throughout Europe and other parts of the world before promoters in the States had the confidence that I could sell out an American concert hall.

With the Queen Mother at the Royal Command Performance.
(Personal collection of Dionne Warwick)

Me and Queen Elizabeth.
(Personal collection of Dionne Warwick)

With Princess Margaret at the Royal Command Performance.
(Personal collection of Dionne Warwick)

This truth didn't leave me angry but, rather, aware. Others were aware, too. This became clear to me after I read a column written by the famed Walter Winchell, who happened to be in my audience at the Olympia Theatre in Paris. He wrote that it was a shame how "another one of our talented performers has had to go overseas to be recognized." His column was widely read and influential, so I thank him for opening the eyes of his readers. It's unfortunate that so many of our African American artists have found moving to other parts of the world the better option for attaining professional success. Why is that? That question still lingers with me, and the answer is still very elusive.

᛫PEAKING OF elusive, hah: for a while, love for me appeared to be elusive. There was that crush I had on Virgil when I was fourteen, and I was engaged for a period of time to Jackie Martin. But because the military was continuously shipping him to God knows where and we were both very young, we both felt it would be best to call off our engagement. And "Then Came You"—the "you" being Mr. Bill Elliott.

I met Bill while doing background on a session with the Rhoda Scott Trio. Bill was the trio's drummer; the other members were Joe Thomas on sax and Rhoda Scott on organ. They were pretty well known up and down the northeastern seaboard and frequently played the local clubs in Newark.

One Newark club where my friends and I would go to hear them play was the Key Club. It was a fun place and had some of the greatest entertainment. People like Arthur Prysock played there. So did organists Jimmy Smith and Richard "Groove" Holmes, and George Benson, who at that time never showed his singing ability but sure let us know he could play guitar.

Bill had a flamboyant personality and was known as "not a one-woman man." He was the "catch," as they say. So I made up my mind to catch him (and I did). After a few months, Bill finally made his move (or so he thought), and to everybody's surprise—including mine—he asked me to marry him.

I brought him home to meet my parents so he could properly ask for my hand. My dad, knowing of Bill's reputation, took him into our living room to have "that" talk. It just so happened that Daddy was getting ready to go on a hunting trip. He was in the process of cleaning his rifle when he asked Bill to join him in the living room. Bill left the living room and the "talk" a bit rattled, to say the least. I found it amusing then and still do. He survived the talk, and so did our relationship. At least for a while.

Bill, a veteran of the navy, loved boats and bought one—from a friend who saw him coming. I am not a boat person in general, and I was wary of the boat that Bill bought. It was a thirty-six-foot, second-, maybe third-hand boat that rarely ran properly, threw smoke when it did run, and could be mistaken for a motorcycle by the sound of its motor. But "Captain" Bill was content with his boat. I never stepped foot on it. He would take it up to Boston, Rhode Island, down to Pittsburgh, and I just know he had to keep his fingers crossed that he would not be lost at sea. Somehow that "chug-a-lug" made it to all of those destinations.

Our wedding was to be held at my parents' home, but on that very day in 1966, Bill decided to take a few of his buddies for a "cruise" that morning. Well, they got stranded in the Hudson River, making him late for the wedding. An hour after the ceremony was supposed to start, I made this announcement: "If he is not here within the next half hour, there will be no wedding!" Bill soon arrived, huffing and puffing, full of apologies, and we got married.

We had moved into our first home, an apartment not far from

my parents. But after three days of marriage, I just woke up and knew I had made a huge mistake. I realized that my flexible freedom of coming and going, which I was accustomed to, would no longer exist. It felt like I had done the wrong thing. In that short period, it seemed like the marriage would have become a mess. To prevent that from happening, I thought it best to do what I did. I woke up Bill and said, "I'll be back." I got on a plane to El Paso, Texas, and caught the "divorce" bus to Juarez, Mexico. It took all of three hours for me to get my "Mexican divorce." I took the bus back to El Paso and flew back to New Jersey a "free" woman. When the divorce decree came in the mail ten days later, I then let Bill know he was a free man again. Yes, he was surprised, but it was too late. I don't know what he thought about my decision, but he made one of his own. He decided a few days later that he wanted to pursue an acting career and headed out to California.

Despite all his efforts to become a working actor, things didn't work out so well, and so Bill went back to doing what he knew best, playing drums. He left Los Angeles, went north to San Francisco, and joined another trio. As fate would have it, in 1967 I was booked to play the Fairmont Hotel in San Francisco. I had not seen or heard from him in months. But, on my opening night, who was sitting front and center but Bill.

After the show, he asked if I'd have a cup of coffee with him. I did, we made small talk, and he asked for the first time why I had divorced him. I let him know I was just not ready to be married. He asked where I was going after San Francisco, and I told him Milan, Italy. Two weeks later, I'm in Milan at the airport, leaving the baggage claim area, when I thought I was seeing things. There stood Bill with a bouquet of flowers. I asked him what he was doing there. He said his sister had married an Italian and was living in Milan. Well, fate was on his side. He also declared that he was going to "woo" me back. I had to admit that this was kinda romantic. And Bill's approach worked. We did still love each other, and the love won out.

Two days later, we remarried in Italy, and this time our marriage lasted for twelve years and blessed us with two sons, David and Damon.

Once back from Italy, I started looking for a home and found it in Maplewood, New Jersey. This particular area boasted a few large estates. I was not looking for a mansion but rather something cozier and more modest—very much like the homes I had grown up in—and I found it: five bedrooms, three bathrooms, a living room. Bill still had aspirations of becoming an actor, but this time he did it properly. He took classes, went out on auditions, and consequently began to get parts in films. He earned a steady role on a TV sitcom called *Bridget Loves Bernie*. This meant he had to go out to Los Angeles, which was the center of the film and TV world. I also ended up in Los Angeles for two reasons: he was there, and much of the record industry had pulled up its stakes in New York and moved to Los Angeles.

I was introduced to a "powerhouse realtor," Elaine Young, and asked her to take me house hunting around LA. She found our house in record time. It was located in the Doheny Estates and was on one of the many bird-named streets. It turned out that my neighbors were all in the entertainment industry: Ray Brown, a sensational bass player, actress Elke Sommer, actor Ricardo Montalban. There was also a lovely couple who lived next door to us, Seymour and Naomi Green. They allowed us to tap into their power lines until we were able to have our power turned on.

Renovation of the house began, and we soon were settled in our new home. It was a bit larger than the home in New Jersey, but the biggest difference was that we had a pool! We were very happy. One of my very best friends lived on Robin Drive as well: Leslie Uggams and her husband, Grahame Pratt, just steps away from our house. We enjoyed wonderful parties and great pinochle games over the years in both of our homes.

All was well until one day, while I was on tour, I received a call from my housekeeper Ree. She had discovered a snake in my closet while cleaning my bedroom. I dropped the phone and had to compose myself before picking it up again for her to also tell me that she had called the ASPCA (American Society for the Prevention of Cruelty to Animals). They put a snake ring around the house, meaning that the snake could not leave the premises even if it wanted to—now, how smart was that?—and they never found the snake. This meant if the snake was still anywhere in or around the house, that was where it was going to stay because it could not cross this device put around the house.

Well, after that there was nothing for me to do but call Elaine and let her know that my house was now on the market. She couldn't believe it. I told Elaine I was selling the house "as is." All the furniture, including the snake, was for sale.

Neither I nor anyone else knew whether "Mr. Snaky Poo" had curled up in one of the sofas, beds, or chairs, or if it had slithered out of the house. All I knew was I was not going to take the chance of possibly transporting it. So I was once again house hunting.

I happened to be pregnant with my second child, Damon, at the time. I began riding around the flats of Beverly Hills when I returned to Los Angeles after my tour, looking at houses, none of which had For Sale signs on them. I finally drove up Elm Drive. I stopped in front of a house that sat on the corner of Elm and Sunset Boulevard. I sat looking at this gorgeous house, and it just seemed to call my name—"Dionne."

I got out of my car, went to the front door, and rang the bell. The lady who answered the door was, ironically, someone I knew,

Helen Noga. She was as surprised to see me as I was to see her. She invited me in and asked what I was doing in Los Angeles. As I was looking around and scoping out the inside of her house, I told her I was house hunting and her house seemed to beckon me. She let out a loud laugh, then asked what did I mean by that. I just blurted out, "I want to buy your house!" Again she laughed and told me her house was not for sale.

I then tried a little psychology on her. I suggested that the house was much too large for just her and her husband, especially since her daughter Beverly and her grandchildren had moved. I also suggested how wonderful it would be for her to sell this house to me so I could raise my young family in it. The look on her face said, "This child is crazy," but I kept talking. She finally said she was not interested in selling her home and wished me luck. Before I left, I gave her my phone number and told her we were staying in a bungalow at the Beverly Hills Hotel. I asked her to think about it.

I had to find a place quickly; it was August already, and registration for school was looking me in the face. David, my eldest son, was now at the age where he was ready to enter school.

Three days later, Helen called me, asking me to come by. She had shared our conversation with her husband, and they had decided to sell their house to me after all. Hooray!

This house, like most of the homes in Los Angeles, was different from any previous place I had called home. It sat on almost an acre of land, had nine bedrooms, which we made into five; seven bathrooms that became five; and a cubbyhole of a kitchen that, since I had begun cooking, soon became a gourmet kitchen. We opened the place up with the renovation, and the house began to take on our personality. The architect was Edward "Ted" Grenzbach, who had designed homes for many in the entertainment world. The interior designer was Joan Schindler.

Since they had renovated our house on Robin Drive, they knew what I wanted and did a wonderful job. They even gave me an office. For what, I don't know. It seemed that every home in Beverly Hills had an office, so now mine did, too.

I was thrilled to discover that Johnny Mathis had lived in this house. Helen Noga was his manager. The beautifully finished basement was used as his rehearsal room. Max Factor, the cosmetics mogul, had originally owned the house, and we were living next door to his granddaughter. She watched as we opened the balconies and archways, returning the house to some of the original grandeur she recalled. We filled in the existing lap pool and moved the new pool to the center of the yard. We restored the tennis court to regulation size. And we gave life back to the orange and lemon trees. Once all was finished, Ms. Factor let me look at a photo of how the original house looked, as evidence of what we had now re-created.

Our home at 806 Elm Drive was always full of kids from the neighborhood, either in the pool or in the kitchen eating things they were not allowed to eat in their homes, such as bologna sandwiches, bacon, and lots of candy, sugar, sugar, and more sugar. All the kids loved our house, and it was our home for the next twenty-five years.

LOOKING BACK at my schedule while I was married, I often wonder how I found time even to sleep, especially during those early years. I traveled and sold out concert halls all over the world. I visited places we all have at one time or another only read about or have seen either in films or on television: Italy, Spain, Germany, Switzerland, England, Ireland, Monte Carlo. And the list of people I met was staggering. Aside from some of the most famous performing artists this world has ever known, I had the pleasure of meeting a multitude of royal families, some of whom I am proud to say I have the privilege to call by their first names, such as His Royal Highness Prince Albert of Monaco.

I also had opportunities that went beyond the concert stage. Film director Herbert Biberman attended a concert I did in upstate New York and after the show came backstage and asked if I would like to be in a film. The project was called *Slaves*. I loved the idea of spreading my wings a bit. So I said yes to his invitation, which would also put me in the company of the awesome actor Ossie Davis in addition to Stephen Boyd, Robert Kya-Hill, and a host of other incredible actors and actresses.

I was to play the character Cassy, the seductive mistress of the slave master MacKay, played by Stephen. I thought being in the movies would be exciting, and it was, in a way. Ossie Davis starred as Luke, the radical slave who was tired of picking "massa's" cotton and leads the other slaves to revolt.

I was scared, though, since the closest thing to a film I had come to was television. But these wonderful actors told me that I had nothing to worry about. They took good care of me.

We shot the film in Shreveport, Louisiana, during July and August of 1968, and it was hot, hot, hot. I was also doing a tour with Cannonball Adderley, Dizzy Gillespie, Thelonious Monk, Nat Adderley, and Ray Brown. I would film Monday through Thursday, fly Friday morning to the show, then fly back to Shreveport Sunday night and start filming the following day. This went on for the entire two months of shooting.

It was hot and I was pregnant, but I got through the filming. And on January 18, 1969, my son David Leland Elliott was born.

Slaves wasn't a hit here in the United States, but it found an audience overseas. The film was even nominated for the Palme d'Or Award at the Cannes Film Festival. *Slaves* was not just a movie to excite or be a commercial hit, it was a work of social commentary.

While it relied on some slave stereotypes, it had a greater purpose: to show how we as a people and as a country got to where we are today and where we had to go in the future.

Nineteen sixty-nine was a banner year for me. Besides giving birth to David, I received my first gold record and won a Grammy for "Do You Know the Way to San Jose." Of course, it was very exciting to get the Grammy and gold record, but both took a backseat to giving birth. I was able to perform during my pregnancy almost to delivery. David was premature and decided he wanted to see

Tearing up after receiving my gold record.
(Personal collection of Dionne Warwick)

the world a little earlier than planned, so there was nothing like a maternity leave. A few months after David was born, I pulled a bit of an industry coup and got my first television special, "The Dionne Warwick Chevy Special." At that time, I was one of the first African American women to host her own television special. My guests were Burt, Glen Campbell, Creedence Clearwater Revival, and impressionist-comedian George Kirby. It was wonderful. Not only did I sing, I danced—finally putting those many hours of dance classes to good use. I even did a skit. I'm proud to say that this accomplishment led to more doors being opened to African American artists in show business.

'VE GOTTEN to know and learn from so many extraordinarily talented icons. And I consider that one of the great blessings of my life. Back in the beginning stages of my career during the '60s, I was the opening act at the Apollo Theater. As I was preparing to go onstage, Ms. Nina Simone was standing in the wings. Although I did not know her that well, she gave me a mantra that I live by to this very day. Nina said to me, with that beautiful tone in her voice, "I want you to go out there and make it very difficult for whoever is following you on that stage. Just know you may be opening the show now—but you are also closing the show." This is a definite piece of advice that I feel could especially benefit those just starting in the business.

Another wonderful woman who gave me words and actions to live by was the great Lena Horne. She told me, "Making promises means you will be constantly tested." And I have been tested, because I constantly seem to be made to put that word *promise* into everything I do. However, the promise she was referring to was the promise to do and be the very best at what I desired to do within this business called show. She said, "Never half-step. Always be prepared to go just a step further than you think you can." She also said, "When you walk on that stage, know that the audience expects you to be more than they came to see and hear." That is the promise I make to every audience that I perform before. Once I enter that stage, I must deliver. I must be doing it right so far; all these years of being an entertainer is a pretty good gauge, I think.

The first time I met Tina Turner was when I was appearing at the Sands Hotel in Las Vegas and she was appearing at the International Hotel. I would rush to change after my performance and get to the International to catch her show nightly. She was, and still is, amazing to watch. After doing her rigorous show, she would graciously greet us backstage to say hello. She also liked to invite us onstage to do one of her closing numbers, usually "Proud Mary." She is still the same lovely, easy person to me that she was way back then.

Aretha Franklin and I met in church while she was on tour with her father, the Reverend C. L. Franklin. She and I were both in our early teens and hit it off immediately; we remain friends to this very day. Ree will always be someone for whom I have a great deal of admiration regarding her talent and her personality. She is not the easiest person to get to know. I think this is because she is basically shy and very private. You really have to be someone she wants to get to know for her to open up. I find this to be an endearing quality. Otherwise, she's funny and witty and has a heart the size of her hometown of Detroit.

I met Patti LaBelle at the Fox Theatre in Brooklyn, New York, back in the '60s. At the time, she was the lead singer for Patti LaBelle and the Bluebelles.

Gladys Knight (whom I call "G") and I met at the Brevoort Theatre in Brooklyn in the early 1960s. We were appearing on the same show, and the Brevoort did not have dressing rooms at that time. So we had to get dressed in the best place we could find: under a stair-well. She would hold up a towel while I got dressed, and I would hold up that same towel for her while she dressed.

We laugh often to this day about that and know that we would probably do it again if need be. G and I are more than friends. She is very much like my sister in every sense of the word. Her mother was like my mom, and my mother was like her mom. We have watched our children grow and get to know one another; we continue to work on projects together; we've been through good times and bad times. We've celebrated together, cried together, and will be as close as we are for as long as we are.

WHENEVER ANY of my icons—Lena Horne, Diahann Carroll, Ella Fitzgerald, Sammy Davis Jr., and Frank Sinatra—played within a hundred-mile radius from me, I did something I don't think any of my peers thought to do: I would go see these icons and "go to class." I would take my legal pad, ask to be seated in the rear of the room with a direct sight line to the stage, and literally take notes.

I wrote down how they entered the stage, how they worked the stage, what they were wearing, how they spoke to the audience, what they said when they spoke to the audience, songs they sang, and how they paced their show.

Diahann Carroll once caught me taking notes. She was perform-ing at the Persian Room in New York in the early '60s. I was seated in the back of the room, busily writing, when all of a sudden I felt the spotlight on my table. When I looked up, she was smiling and said, "Little girl, what are you doing?"

After I stammered an answer that nobody heard but me, she said, "Please speak up." Completely embarrassed, I answered. She then asked me to come to her suite after the show and to bring "my notes."

I was escorted to her suite with my pad in hand. I sat nervously waiting for her. She entered and said, "May I see your notes, little girl?" I gave her the pad, and she began to laugh out loud as she read them. "You have written everything that I did in my show," she said. "Why?"

I told her she was doing something that I wanted to do eventually and playing the places that I hoped to play and that she apparently was doing what it took to get to that level. I considered her show a class where I could go to study. She said, "I think you will not only play the places that I play but will also go even further." To this very day, she still calls me "little girl."

Diahann is the "ultimate glamour girl." I learned a lot from her. She is someone who insisted that I be "camera ready," even if I was going to the grocery store. Diahann said—and it's true—that "the public has a perception of who you are and are constantly looking to see you present yourself as they perceive you in their mind." I've told so many people, "I don't get up the way people think, in full makeup, every hair in place, dressed to the nines." I let them know I am as human as they are, and my mornings start with every hair out of place, too.

One thing Diahann said that I do keep in mind is that it is all done with "smoke and mirrors." Even when wearing a pair of jeans, if you wear them with a pair of heels instead of sneakers, you are making a fashion statement. And you know what? She is right. I've felt comfortable going into some of the swankiest restaurants wearing jeans, a crisp white shirt, a blazer, and heels.

Sammy Davis Jr. was a glorious human being whom I remember with deep, heartfelt emotion. He was always kind and quick to smile. He was a terrible poker player, though, and an even worse Ms. Pacman player. He came to see me once at the Sands Hotel in Las Vegas, giving me compliments and tips. He told me that I should be announced before I enter the stage. Well, I felt there was no need to be introduced, since everyone in the room knew who they had come to see. He felt there might be a few who did not know who they were seeing, and so the next show I let the audience know that *Sammy Davis Jr.* felt I should have an introduction. So I introduced myself and let the audience know as well that I was not Ann-Margret. Well, Sammy came backstage later to say that I should also consider becoming a comedian.

I miss him a lot, as we spent some really wonderful quality time together, and I could fill dozens of notepads with what I learned from his shows. Sammy Davis Jr. is the greatest entertainer who ever lived.

Frank Sinatra, whom I affectionately called "Poppy," was like a surrogate father and proved to be one of the kindest and most personable people that I have ever met. I was a bit afraid to meet him initially. His reputation preceded him. But once I did, I came away with an opinion of him that was much different from what I had heard. He always made himself available to me whenever I needed him to be a part of any of my charitable projects. In turn, I made sure I was available whenever he needed me to do any work for his charities.

His words of wisdom for me were "Always be honest with your audience." I did not know exactly what he meant at the time. But later I would understand that an audience can feel that you are giving your all and when what you do comes from your heart. While I was hosting the show *Solid Gold* in 1986 (my second time as the show's host), I asked him to be one of my guests. When I first brought up the possibility, the powers that be snickered and said, "Yeah, right." I got a bit angry that they did not believe I could get him to do the show.

Well, when the day that Frank was to do the show came, those "suits," still looking at me as if I had two more heads on my shoulders, remained in disbelief. People at Paramount came out of the woodwork to see if this was really going to happen. I was so happy to look at them all and say, "Are you convinced now?" The show was wonderful. I performed a duet with him, "You and Me," which I have in my personal archive.

I wasn't so bothered by the industry execs having their doubts. I have always been motivated by people who tell me what I can't do. It happened the first time I played the world-famous Copacabana in New York in the late '60s. First of all, I was thrilled to step onto the same stage as the best of the best had: Sammy, Frank, Ella Fitzgerald, Sarah Vaughan. It was more than any dream I ever had. So when I got there, I employed one of the lessons I learned from another of my role models: Johnny Mathis.

He would enter the stage without fanfare and sing for what seemed like an hour before he said a word to his audience. He began with a medley of his hits and mesmerized everyone in that room. I said to myself, *One day I am going to do that, too.*

By the time my Copacabana engagement arrived, I put together a medley of songs that ran close to fifteen minutes, and I opened the show sitting on a stool and singing the medley. I was so very proud to be able to do this, and I received a standing ovation. After the show, this young man was brought to my dressing room and introduced to me as Barbra Streisand's manager. Without a pause, he said I could not just walk onto a stage and sing for fifteen minutes without greeting my audience. He kinda ticked me off, and after he finished, I simply said to him, "Apparently you were in the audience, and what you are saying I can't do you watched me do." I also let him know that he should give advice to the one he was managing.

A similar thing happened when I played the Apollo Theater. The show was called Coming Home and featured my church choir, the New Hope Baptist Young Adult Choir; the Emotions (a wonderful group of sisters, and fabulous singers); my sister, Dee Dee; and comedian Redd Foxx. It was a show that brought "downtown" "uptown"—meaning that people from downtown Manhattan, who would not normally come uptown to Harlem, came to see this amazing show. So I was very excited.

I decided to do the song "People." Bobby Schiffman, the owner of the Apollo at that time, heard me rehearse it and told me that I shouldn't sing the song. He thought the audience would not appreciate it. Well, smoke came out of my ears. I had no intention of not singing the song, and when I did, I let the audience know I was told not to sing this song but felt if I could do it at the Copa, why not at the Apollo? At the end of the evening, Bobby was the one to let me know that the standing ovation I received lasted for three minutes. He apologized for second-guessing me.

I've never felt the pressure to prove anything to anyone or to defer to someone else when I already had a clear vision about what I was doing artistically. But despite my experience and my accomplishments, people have asked me to prove myself over and over again. And that continues to amaze me.

I learned valuable lessons about separating my personal life from my public life. It's allowed me to keep a level head in spite of criticism and in spite of betrayal. Some of the betrayal I've experienced has also come from the media.

Some say that publicity, good or bad, is necessary for success in the entertainment world. I always felt that I give so much of me to "John Q. Public" that there has to be just a bit of me that I should keep for myself.

I was once burned by an interview I granted to a New York newspaper. The story was to run in conjunction with my appearance at Lincoln Center. A reporter (I have chosen not to remember his name) followed me for three days. I took him to some of my friends' homes, some of the little clubs we frequented, and even invited him into my parents' home, where he put his feet under my mother's dining room table and broke bread with us.

This man then wrote an article that was so degrading it took me more than twenty years before I would consent to another in-depth interview. He was so disrespectful in the way he described my friends and their homes. I took him to the places we went to hear great music and have fun—and no, they were not places like the Copa or the Persian Room. He was a guest in my family's home and ate every bit of the meal my mother had prepared. If he is still alive, he should know I will never forgive him for how he portrayed it all. (I'd really like to say something else, but I wish to remain the lady I was taught to be.) The legendary singer Nina Simone taught me a lesson to remember about doing an interview, though. She said to always have a tape recorder running while doing interviews so that "what is said is what is printed." That has stuck with me. And I share this little tidbit with all who may have to be interviewed for any reason, especially those of you in the public eye for whom being interviewed is a part of your job.

Success is also so unpredictable. It can overwhelm a person like the waves of the ocean. Or it can happen as it did in my case (like a steady stream flowing over many years). I'm glad it happened like that because it allowed me to be able to deal with those peaks and valleys.

I was one of the lucky ones. Part of the reason is that I remained *me* among my friends, family, and all who knew me. In contrast, I have watched so many of my professional peers become someone they weren't, letting this thing called stardom go completely to their heads. It doesn't have to be that way.

For those who have aspirations of becoming a part of show business, know that it takes a wealth of hard work, and earning longevity is not an easy thing to accomplish. It takes dedication to your craft. Being prepared is the first order of business. So you have to sort out what that will mean for you. I was blessed with a natural gift and have never taken a formal vocal lesson. However, many people benefit greatly from formal training. It's important for aspiring singers to find out what works best for them and to be original. Also, know that there may be rejections along the way, but if it is your dream and is what you most desire, continued fortitude, broad shoulders, and true dedication will see you through.

Know who you can trust—and I mean have complete trust in. And make sure it's someone who will be curious enough to ask questions on your behalf and get answers; someone you know will absolutely have you and your best interest at heart. These kinds of folks (if you are lucky enough to have one in your life) will help to keep everyone you do business with "on the good foot."

DIONNE'S LESSONS LEARNED

- *Be and let be.*

- *Love can be elusive.*

- *Always be honest. (Find someone you can trust.)*

- *Change is caused by circumstances.*

- *Be prepared.*

- *Follow your dreams; dedication will see you through.*

- *Perfect the craft of giving audiences more than what is expected of you.*

CHAPTER 4

Walk On By

I N 1971 I made my last recording for Scepter Records. Florence would soon be closing its doors, and I felt like I was being forced to leave my mother and sent to live with an uncle I did not know. Nevertheless, I signed with Warner Bros. Records, where Mo Ostin was the CEO and Joe Smith was president, and I was promised the world: the same care that was given to me at Scepter. They said I would be well promoted, produced at the same high level, and given the full support of concerts.

Unfortunately, that is not how it turned out. I was at Warner Bros. for around four years and recorded five albums with the best producers in the business: Thom Bell, Jerry Ragovoy, Michael Omartian, and Steve Barri, and the team of Brian Holland, Lamont Dozier, and Eddie Holland. Unfortunately, these albums seemed to be a well-kept secret from the public. Warners did not promote the albums, and the reason why is a mystery to me. Now, if they were really bad recordings, which they were not, then I could understand.

But that clearly wasn't the case. My first album for Warners, titled *Dionne,* has wonderful songs, wonderful producers, and all of the ingredients of a well-done project. But even the very best recordings don't become hits on their own. They have to have the promotional muscle of the company to push the product, and for that, the company has to believe in the product. But apparently Warners did not believe in this product.

You may wonder why I was suddenly working with different producers. When I moved to Warners, I felt comfortable knowing that Burt and Hal would continue writing and producing for me. For years, I heard from disc jockeys who said that Bacharach, David, and Warwick were a "marriage made of music." As I mentioned before, I often described us as "the triangle marriage that worked," and soon that's how the industry thought of us, too. But the triangle marriage stopped working at a point. Friendships are built over time. And all whom I consider friends have been with me from childhood right up to this very moment and have been there for me when I needed them. Friends are more like family, people you can depend on. I consider it a privilege to have as many friends as I do. So when things began to unravel between me, Burt, and Hal, whom I considered my friends, I was caught by surprise.

As I later learned, a few months after I joined Warners, there were rumblings going on in the Bacharach and David camp. I had no knowledge of this at first and found out later, exactly the way the rest of the world did: I read it in the music trade papers. My father had heard about this through the grapevine and had tried to forewarn me. I told him it could not be true; if it were, Burt and Hal would have told me. But it was true. I suddenly found myself at a new record label without familiar writers and producers. I felt betrayed and hurt.

From what I understood, the breakup was caused over the music score for a movie titled *Lost Horizons.* It was a case of Burt having to redo the score and Hal leaving for vacation while Burt did this alone. I know, it sounds petty. Years later, I asked Burt about it, and he said he felt that we had already had our run (which is a crock). So to this day, I'm still not sure if this is the whole story behind the breakup.

Nevertheless, this was a stressful time in my life, since the three of us had signed the contract with Warner Bros., and their departure put us in breach of that contract. If Bacharach and David were not speaking to each other, there was no way that they would be able to write together, which left me like a fish out of water. After the three of us missed a recording deadline, I was asked to come to Mo Ostin's office to discuss what could be done to get recording plans back on track. I really did not have much of a solution to this huge problem. Mo suggested that the situation would probably result in a lawsuit, meaning that Warner Bros. would have to sue me. I was pregnant with my second child and thought I would go into labor right then and there. Just imagine being told that big Warner Bros. might have to sue little me. Knowing the relationship that Burt, Hal, and I had, Mo asked if I thought I could persuade them to get together to write. I thought there was no way they were going to get together to write anything. But I agreed to give it a try.

Burt was appearing in Lake Tahoe at Harrah's at this time, and Mo arranged for me to take one of Warner's private planes there to talk with him. Hal and his family were in Israel on vacation and would be returning sometime during that week. Off I flew to Lake Tahoe and sat through Burt's show, trying to think of the approach I would take. Afterward, I went backstage to his dressing room and just blurted out that we were in serious trouble with the record company and that if he and Hal did not get together very soon, we were in for a major lawsuit. To my surprise, this did not seem to bother him at all. He just flat-out said there is no way that he and Hal would be getting together to do anything.

The flight back to Los Angeles the next morning was the longest ever. I met with Mo later that afternoon with the not-so-good news, and he repeated that Warner might start legal proceedings against the three of us. He did offer an alternative, and that was for *me* to sue Burt and Hal, since they were my producers and were in breach of contract with me. I felt quite relieved to know they were on the hook and not me. So I sued them both. We settled out of court, and the outcome will never be known beyond the parties involved.

The three of us didn't speak for the next twelve years. We had to work hard at times not to cross one another's paths. We were still obliged to attend the same industry functions. It was very awkward, especially since photographers and news media wanted our photos or comments on the matter.

Burt and I even performed on the same television special during the heart of the breakup. What a cat-and-mouse game we played to avoid running into each other. And to make matters worse, our dressing rooms were next to each other. I wasn't sure if I saw Burt that I could just walk on by, in the words of the song. So I asked my wardrobe lady to hang out near my dressing room door and alert me to when he was coming out of his dressing room. We never actually ran into each other, which I consider a blessing.

There was another similar incident at the Roxy club in Los Angeles. Burt had just married songwriter Carole Bayer Sager, and she was promoting her album there. Her special guest was Christopher Cross. I was being devilish and thought it would be fun to go with a few of my friends. They sat us right up front, where neither Carole nor Burt could miss us. Burt caught sight of me in the audience from the backstage area where he stood. Not only did I see him, but my entire table did, too. Unlike Burt, Hal at least called me shortly after the settlement to say how sorry he was about what had happened. The silence wasn't broken between Burt and me until a television project called *Finder of Lost Loves,* an Aaron Spelling production. Burt was asked to write the theme song for the show, and Aaron insisted that he ask me to sing it. When he called and said, "It's Burt," I said, "Burt who?" But I did agree to meet him at my home. I braced myself, and when he arrived, he hurried to his "security blanket"— my piano—and started to play the song. As I started to sing, he finally said those three words that I had been waiting for: "I am sorry." I remembered Mo saying to me long ago that if anyone could mend the fence between us, it would be me. And I did. Burt and Hal wrote a song for me again, the first song they had written in seventeen years. The song was called "Sunny Weather Lover."

A MAJOR CHANGE took place in my life in 1973. Not only was my second son, Damon, born, my marriage to his father, Bill, ended. Home life and career were good but had begun to take a toll on my marriage. Being on tour as much as I was gave Bill the opportunity to return to old bad habits. Twelve years into our marriage, it seemed that everyone but me knew he was playing the field and had a few women chasing after him.

This was confirmed when I actually saw him with one of these women.

I had been shopping in Beverly Hills and decided to stop for a cup of coffee, and there he was, in the same place, with this woman having what appeared to be an intimate moment. I walked up behind him and tapped him on the shoulder. I really wanted to hurt him. Instead I said, "Hi, Bill. 'Bye, Bill." He filed for divorce this time and thought he was going to get custody of our two boys. I brought a lot of drama and much ado in the courtroom, to the

My husband, Bill Elliott, and I with nephew Barry and son David at the circus.
(Personal collection of Dionne Warwick)

point where the judge almost charged me with contempt of court. But at the end of the day, I got my name back and custody. Bill was granted visitation rights, but the boys would remain in my care. The divorce was granted in December 1975.

Sadly, Bill passed away a couple of years later from a massive heart attack. He had gone his way and I mine, but I had his body shipped back to his home, Baltimore, where he received a military burial. I felt this was the least that I could do for his mother and his family, and for David and Damon.

Although I was recording, my music was no longer getting the airplay that it had in previous years. When I wasn't on the road, I took this as an opportunity to be with my family, sleep in my own bed for a change, and hang with my friends. The declining popularity of my work proved to be not so bad after all. I became a "normal person." I carpooled my children and their friends to school and activities. I prepared meals for my family. I had time to go to the playground with my children and their friends and play cards with my buddies—all a nice reprieve from being on the road.

Eventually, though, I had to go back to work. And I soon learned that I still had many loyal friends (fans) who continued to support me. However, the road was not as much fun as it used to be but, rather, a necessity to keep the lights on and a roof over our heads. I was starting all over again in many ways. I was a newly single mother, and that was a challenge. But I had two wonderful sons whom I adored. The unconditional love between us is what kept me together physically and emotionally.

Every day, I thank God for my children.

There were changes in my life that I couldn't control, but there were other changes that I made voluntarily—even if years later I don't really know why—such as adding the letter *e* to my last name. Maybe it had something to do with making a fresh start.

I had met a wonderful astrologer and renowned author, Linda Goodman, in the early part of the '70s. We struck up a fun-filled friendship, and at some point she did my chart, which I still have and still don't know how to read.

In addition to my astrological chart, she did a numerological one. And that's where the idea of adding an *e* to the end of my surname came from: to create "stronger vibrations." Linda suggested it, and I did not see any harm in it. Little did I know the chaos it would cause my attorney, agents, promoters, and record company, especially once I changed it legally to "Warwicke." That meant that every contract, advertisement, and record cover had to reflect the change. For those who are interested, feel free to look up some of the Warner Bros. records, and you'll see the *e* is there.

Linda may be a terrific astrologer, but I don't know about the numerology. That *e* seemed to cause (I think it was the *e)* all hell to break loose in my life. I went through two divorces, the first from my husband, and the second from Bacharach and David. My record sales declined. Yep, I blamed it on that *e,* and I went about getting it taken off all contracts, marquees, and future album covers. That caused grumbling all over again—but it was done.

People have often said to me, "Boy, would I love to trade places with you." I in turn ask them if they think they could deal with my daily schedule for a week, much less a lifetime. They say yes, until I describe a typical three-day schedule:

Pack both travel wear and performance wear for a three-day weekend going through three different temperature changes. Car pickup at four thirty in the morning. Airplane leaves at six or seven; travel time usually four to five hours. Arrive at first destination, check into hotel. Sound check (meaning run through the material and test the microphone to make sure everything is working and sounding properly). Back to hotel to shower, do makeup and hair. (No, I don't have a "glam squad." I do these things myself.) Back to the venue for the performance, which is usually over around ten thirty. Back to the hotel; wake-up call at four to make a seven o'clock flight to the next place. Another three- to four-hour flight. Arrive at second destination. Check into hotel. Go to sound check. Back to the hotel. Again. And again. And this goes on practically every weekend, not to mention the many one-nighters when I'm on a full-fledged tour. After hearing all this, the same people usually say, "Maybe I *don't* want to trade places with you."

A career in entertainment is anything but easy. There is the preparation, the travel, the performance, and then there are the interviews, press conferences, and television appearances that promoters all expect you to do on the day you arrive at some of the places where you'll be performing that evening. Youngsters in the business today would turn up their noses at my schedule and probably insist that promoters know there has to be at least two days between performances. Ah, the luxury of being new to the game.

When my career declined, I set a new goal for myself. I decided to go back to school to earn a master's degree in music.

I asked one of my professors, Dr. Joe Mulready, if he would come out on the road and tutor me, and he agreed. It worked out fine. The music that I was recording of Burt Bacharach's was not the easiest to sing, and what I learned in the course of earning a music degree helped me to better perform the melodies he wrote. The time signature changes that Burt wrote within the body of the songs, the shifting intervals of notes, were meant to convey the emotions evoked by the beautiful lyrics Hal wrote. I used to feel like I was taking an exam each time we went into the studio. I sometimes thought that Burt would think to himself, *Let's see if she can handle this one.*

Most people aren't aware of my musical training. I took piano lessons every week from the age of six until my early twenties. My parents insisted that I practice one hour every day. As a teenager, I was the pianist for the Gospelaires. I learned how to read music for both piano and voice, which gave me a huge advantage over many of my contemporaries. I was able to sight-read the music charts. I also have relative pitch. If, for example, someone were to play a C note, I could sing an E note simultaneously—without that note being played.

Despite all of this early training, I felt there was room to perfect my musical craft. My inspiration to go back to school was Dr. Roberta Flack. Roberta is a wonderful singer, with hits such as "The First Time Ever I Saw Your Face" and "Feel Like Makin' Love." She is also a professor of music and was always an example of what and how music should be presented: in a word, *perfection.* It is never too late to become a student of your craft. To be the best "ain't such a bad thing."

And it's never too late to learn more about business, either. Until a few years ago, the meaning of "global brand" was all new to me. I had to begin to think of myself as a global brand. Little did I know until recently the importance of being a "brand." I have learned from the "babies," as I call them: the young professionals reigning in the business today.

However, in the '80s, I was among the first artists to develop a fragrance. It was called Dionne. We held a party at Stringfellows, a plush club in New York City, to celebrate my fragrance launch at Macy's department stores. Both Andy Warhol and I had a wonderful time at the party. Andy and I spoke about my music and how much he enjoyed it. He also wanted to know if I would like to have one of his portraits from the multicolor series that he was doing at that time. Unfortunately, he passed before he was able to do this. Andy was a very soft-spoken, gentle man.

Andy Warhol and me: Andy attended my fragrance launching party
at Stringfellows in New York City. (Getty Images)

I'm currently involved with a wonderful doctor, Veronica Lazarus, in creating a skin care line for men and women of color. I am in partnership with a fabulous interior designer, Bruce Garrick. I'm also in the process of putting together a one-woman show with hopes of bringing it to Broadway. In 2008 my first children's book was published, *Say a Little Prayer*. I had a wonderful time promoting that book. I'm also working on a few literary ventures as an author. In addition to the above, I have several other major projects in development, not to mention my personal appearance schedule. So yes, I'm busy. However, I continue to repeat my grandfather's words: "If you can think it, you can do it."

DIONNE'S LESSONS LEARNED

- *True friendship never really ends.*

- *A lull in employment can be a period of personal growth.*

- *Nothing beats a failure but a try.*

- *It's never too late to be a student.*

- *Being the best ain't such a bad thing.*

CHAPTER 5

Heartbreaker

WHEN 1976 rolled around, I was no longer with Warner Bros. Records, nor was I signed to any other record company. I was asked to do *The Dinah Shore Show,* and one of the other guests was an old friend, Clive Davis, a music industry legend. It had been a while since I had seen him. Backstage, we were catching up on what was happening in our lives when he let me know that he had just started a new label and was having great success with Barry Manilow. He also asked what record label I was on. I explained that with what was going on then, with all the disco-type music, there did not seem to be a place for me. Therefore, I was considering dusting off my credentials—having earned both bachelor's and master's degrees in music—and giving teaching a try, since the music industry seemed not to want me anymore. Just think, if my life had taken a turn to teaching, this might have been the last chapter of this book. But God had other plans for me.

Barry Manilow and me.
(Personal collection of Dionne Warwick)

Clive said that while I might be ready to give up the industry, the industry was not ready to give up me. He asked if I would consider coming to his label, Arista Records. I must say I was hesitant because of my past experience at Warner Bros. I told him I would think about it. He let me know the door was open, and whenever I wanted to discuss this possibility, to just let him know.

I gave it some long, hard thought and felt it was worth a discussion. Ultimately, I said yes. It was probably one of the best decisions I ever made. I signed with Arista and began to talk with people there about songs, writers, and producers. And since Barry was having great success at Arista as an artist, writer, and producer, Clive thought he would be a candidate to write for and produce me. The writing part was appealing, but I had to think about the producer part. Barry Manilow produced himself well, but could he produce me as well or better? You see, as an artist, you need to have a rapport with your producer in order to create a great record. I went to Barry's home in Los Angeles for our first musical meeting to choose songs, and I was truly impressed to find that he had done his homework. On his piano was something that *I* did not have: every album that I had ever recorded. He told me how he, Bette Midler, and Melissa Manchester used to listen to me and get inspiration from my records. After a few meetings, Barry convinced me that he was the person for this project.

This started a long-lasting friendship and led to my first recording for Arista and my first platinum recording, *Dionne.* Not only did *Dionne* sell more than a million copies, in 1979 I won Grammy Awards in the two highest categories, Best R&B Vocal Performance, Female, for "Déjà Vu" (my gift from Isaac Hayes), and Best Contemporary Vocal Performance, Female, for "I Know I'll Never Love This Way Again." It just goes to show that you can't judge a book by its cover. It's impossible for me to describe what it feels like to win a Grammy Award. Knowing your peers have decided that you were the best in your category represents the icing on the cake of a successful career. Knowing that I, like Ella Fitzgerald, won two awards, and to be part of Grammy history (as the first female solo artist to receive Grammy Awards in pop and R&B categories in the same year) made the acknowledgment even sweeter. Over my career, I have been nominated for thirteen Grammy Awards and won five.

Winning Grammys also opened up other doors. In 1979 I received a call from Bob Banner, the renowned television producer, asking if I'd be interested in cohosting a musical special with Glen Campbell. The show would be sort of a prelude to the Grammys and would feature the hit recordings of the time. It was called *Solid Gold.*

It was a bunch of fun working with Glen, and a solid friendship began. The show was such a hit that Paramount Studios decided to make it a series. The show was an experience of music, dance, and laughter and ran from 1980 through 1988. We were rated the number one variety show nationwide, and what I loved most about the show was that the entire family could enjoy it together. I remember being at the checkout counter in a supermarket in Los Angeles one evening when I noticed the lady in front of me was becoming a bit anxious and seemed to want to get out of the store in a hurry. I felt the need to say something, so I said, "They sure are slow." And she turned to me and said, "Yes, they are. And they are going to make me late to see *Solid Gold.*" I just lowered my head and smiled.

It was and still is a great feeling to know how much people really enjoyed the show. I hosted the first and fifth seasons. While doing it, I had the pleasure of getting to know some brilliant new talent and the chance to work with some of my peers. Some of the entertainers who appeared on *Solid Gold* were Phil Collins, Stevie Wonder, the Charlie Daniels Band, Billy Dee Williams, Michael McDonald, Peter Frampton, Boy George, Sister Sledge, Whitney Houston, James Ingram, Jose Feliciano, Billy Preston, Stanley Clarke and George Duke, Arsenio Hall, and Little Richard.

OVER THE years, I have had the pleasure of performing many types of music, in some of the best venues in the world. The first time I appeared at Carnegie Hall was shortly after the 1965 passing of musical legend Nat "King" Cole. It was to do a fund-raiser for cancer organized by Maria Cole for her late husband. Every name act who knew Nat personally was there to pay tribute. There was laughter from the comedy stars he worked with, and there was plenty of music from his peers, including me. I did not have the pleasure of knowing him the way all of the others did, but I sure knew his music, and it was such an awesome pleasure to have been included to pay homage to him in such a grand and festive way.

I next appeared at Carnegie Hall with jazz great Stan Getz. I was on tour with Stan, and to do my thirty minutes in front of him was the thrill of my life. I guess I had practiced enough. (You know the old joke: "How do you get to Carnegie Hall?" "Practice.") Since then, I have performed there doing my own show, and each time it is the very same thrill. Carnegie Hall is probably one of the most prestigious concert halls on the planet. So if you are lucky enough to be invited to perform there, you can let the world know that you have arrived.

In the early '80s, I was asked to perform at another prestigious venue. It was the annual concert Christmas in Vienna with Plácido Domingo. I immediately said yes. I was so excited. I was flown to Vienna, Austria, for rehearsals with the Vienna Boys' Choir, the Vienna Symphony Orchestra, and, of course, with opera icon Plácido. It was a wonderful three days spent with this most impressive cast of musicians and singers. The trip was also filmed, and scenes recorded included visits to restaurants, the Christmas market, and the concert that was held in the wonderful city hall.

I was invited to do the concert again. This would be Plácido's last time hosting Christmas in Vienna. He had been asked to be the head of an American opera company and had accepted the position. Plácido is currently the general director of the Los Angeles Opera and the Washington National Opera. The second time was as thrilling as the first. The first show sold enough CDs and DVDs to earn platinum status in sales. I am hopeful that they will reinstitute this event, as it really depicted what I had always thought the celebration and the holiday spirit of Christmas is all about.

I had the pleasure of performing twice for the Christmas at the Vatican concerts during the time of Pope John Paul II. He was a very gentle man with an enormous presence. These shows were absolutely glorious. The talent came from all parts of the world, giving me an opportunity to meet some very special people. I had the pleasure of taking my mother with me to one of the performances, and before we did the shows, we were all invited to meet the Pope. I am not Catholic, but this was nonetheless a very special experience for me. All of us who performed on the show gathered in a hall designated for this meeting to receive a blessing from him. He laid his hands on my mom, which brought her to tears. And when he touched my hand, I felt why he was called "His Holiness."

A funny thing happened the first time I met the Pope. We were all standing in the hall waiting for him. I was asked by some of my friends if I would have him bless their crosses, so I was standing there with about seven of them in my hand. As he got closer to me, I started arranging the crosses so that he would touch each of them. Well, he came to me, and as I stuck my hand out holding the crosses, he just said, "Bless you, my child." I could not let him not bless these crosses, so I broke rank and ran to the end of the line, and as he got closer to me, he had this smile on his face. I said, "I know you have blessed me already, but will you please bless these crosses?" I'm happy to say he did and made many people very happy. And I got a double blessing as he again said to me, "Bless you, my child." I will always remember his smile and his calm presence.

WAS RAISED listening to all kinds of music, including classical, and have loved working with artists in the classical world such as José Carreras and Andrea Bocelli. I have also appeared with the Opera Company of Japan. Something that few people are aware of is that the legendary opera singer Leontyne Price is my cousin. Her relationship to me is from my mother's side of the family. Leontyne lived in the South and was not constant in my life. But when we see each other at functions, we'll acknowledge each other with "Hey, cuz."

Jazz is another form of music that I love to sing. I worked with "Count" Basie, whom I met by way of my longtime dear friend Pam Jackson. He is her godfather. Working with him was a blast. He was a very gentle and funny man who always had a smile on his face and a joke to tell. I sang with Joe Williams, a thrilling experience because he's an amazing artist, and I later found out that we shared a birthday (December 12). We appeared together the first time on a 1976 television show called "The Original Rompin', Stompin' Hot and Heavy, Cool and Groovy All-Star Jazz Show." Now, if that's not a mouthful, I don't know what is. The show was absolutely wonderful. Every jazz great you can think of performed: Joe, Stan Getz, Herbie Hancock, Lionel Hampton, Dizzy Gillespie, Gerry Mulligan, Max Roach—all hosted by little ol' me, my mouth being wide open with joy at being in this kind of company. (The George Faison Dancers were also featured.) The next time I had the opportunity to sing with Mr. Williams was at a benefit in Los Angeles. He passed away shortly thereafter, I'm sad to say.

Back in the late '60s, I worked on a special with the great Duke Ellington while in South America. What an honor it is to say Duke Ellington played piano for me. He was very kind and told me I had great potential. I took this to mean that I had to do a lot more practicing to reach the standard of singers he was accustomed to working with, such as Billie Holiday, Sarah Vaughan, and Ella Fitzgerald, to mention a few. And at this point in my career, I am still practicing to come up to those standards.

I have been fortunate to have had many mentors: Sammy

Davis Jr., Frank Sinatra ("Poppy"), Marlene Dietrich and Lena Horne (my mother allowed me to call both of these ladies "Momma"), Ella Fitzgerald, and, of course, Sarah "Sassy" Vaughan. "Aunt Sass," as I called her, grew up with my mom and was always around our home. She was relatively quiet, and just being around her and listening to her sing—her phrasing of lyrics, her intonation, and her choice of songs—gave me great insight into how to approach a lyric and how to use the music vocally, an education you can't get in a classroom.

Johnny Mathis is another one from whom I learned well. I refer to John's voice as "velvet." The way he caresses a lyric, his tonality, his bigger-than-life-stage presence—not to mention his good looks—can be overshadowed only by his personality. He is an extremely kind, giving, gentle man, and he also knows his way around a kitchen. Yep, he is a chef-caliber cook. I have firsthand knowledge. I've had the extreme pleasure of touring with him, recording with him, and I guess I can say just flat out having fun with him.

It wasn't until I slowed down to write this book that I realized I've known some of these people for nearly fifty years. Where did the time go?

Marvin Gaye and I met in the early '60s, when we were doing a record hop together. A record hop was a form of promotion we all did for disc jockeys around the country, especially those who were playing our records. It was much like doing *Bandstand,* but on a smaller, local scale. They were usually held in ballrooms filled with kids who were record buyers, and we would perform our recordings live for them. It was a lot of fun, since most of the kids were our age, and we related to them with no problem.

Marvin was one of those people you could not help but admire. He was smooth, very good looking, and had a voice like no other. The record hop Marvin and I did was to promote our first recordings: his "Stubborn Kind of Fellow" and mine, "Don't Make Me Over." It was in Detroit, and the DJ who was promoting the hop was Ernie Durham. We did more of these together because our records were released almost simultaneously. Marvin and I soon became friends.

Diana Ross and I met in Miami, Florida, where I was playing in a club at the Sir John Hotel. The Motown Revue was in town. On my night off, I went to see the show and went backstage to say hi to Marvin Gaye, Smokey Robinson, the Contours, and Kim Weston, all of whom I had worked with in theaters around the country. They introduced me to the girls, and we hit it off great. It seemed like a magic wand hung over Motown Records and all of its artists. There was not a place in the world where I didn't hear a Motown artist's record.

The Supremes—Florence, Mary, and Diana—were the queens of the airwaves. They began traveling in the same circle as I was, and we would cross paths frequently. As a result, I could see when things began to change for this girl group. I, like quite a few people, also noticed the difference being made between the three ladies. When the group's name was changed to Diana Ross and the Supremes in 1967, it was the buzz of the industry. In January 1970, Diana left the group and was launched as a solo act immediately. Unfortunately, Diana Ross's reputation preceded her. She never showed me what could be described as her "demanding and self-indulgent side," but behavior that could be described as such was documented. I recently saw her in Saks in Beverly Hills. She looked great and was very excited to tell me that her daughter Rhonda had made her a grandmother. We chatted about how my children were as well and hugged before we went our merry ways.

ANOTHER THING that made the '60s such fun for me was appearing on Danny Thomas's television show. In addition to having a hit program at the time, Danny was a very successful television producer. He also founded the St. Jude Children's Research Hospital in Tennessee. Early in my career, Danny was very helpful to me. He was also very kind. I not only sang on his show, but he also put me in comedy sketches. I will always remember how he protected all that appeared on his show, never letting something go on air if it could be done better. He told me I had a flair for comedy and should do more of it. I appeared on his show several times, and he and his wife, Rose Marie, decided that I was a part of the family. I lived close to his home in Beverly Hills, and they often invited me to dinner. When Terre, one of their daughters, was about to have her baby, she decided that if it was a girl she would name her Dionne. Turns out, it was a girl, and her name is Dionne, and this let me know how much this family really loved me.

One of my dearest friends and someone else I loved hanging out with was Phil Ramone. He is known throughout the entire world as one of the premier recording engineer-producers, having overseen countless hit records by Billy Joel, Paul McCartney, Paul Simon, and Frank Sinatra, to name a few. He engineered the majority of my recordings from 1965 through 1972 at his independent studio A&R Recording in New York City. Phil is a musician, which made it easier for the producers because he could follow a score, and when asked to go to a certain part of the music, he could do it with ease. He had and still has the ability to mix while recording, which gives everyone a chance to hear what the finished recording would probably sound like. We are still very close friends, and whenever I have the chance to record with him, it is a complete pleasure.

I also had a wonderful time working with the man Frank Sinatra dubbed "the Voice," Tony Bennett. He is someone who easily smiles, has a kind word for all he meets, and treated me like a princess. Tony has always had nothing but very inspiring and good things to say about my voice, and working with him has been and will always be a joy.

One of my very best friends is Nancy Wilson. She is known as "Sweet Nancy," and I can attest to this title as being completely accurate in describing her. She is elegant, attractive, and, yes, can truly sing! Her voice and phrasing have always reminded me of another singer, "Little" Jimmy Scott—one of her favorite singers. I've spent a lot of time with her in my home, in her home, through the births of her children, and she through the births of mine. We are both pinochle players and have enjoyed many an evening that turned into the next day playing with my other pinochle buddies, Leslie Uggams and Mira Waters. We will always be friends.

Another person very dear to my heart is legendary singer Chuck Jackson. He was a label mate of mine while I was at Scepter Records. Chuck recorded hits such as "Any Day Now" and "I Don't Want to Cry," and, like the rest of the roster there, he became family. I am very happy to say that he is still in great health, and his voice is better than ever. I always look forward to being with him and his wife, Helen. He has the reputation of also being a great cook, but, unfortunately, he has yet to cook for me. (That's a hint, Chuck.)

I met Tom Jones while doing the TV show *Ready Steady Go!* in London in the early '60s, and we became instant friends. One very cold and wintry night when I had just finished a recording session and pulled my car out of the garage on Fifty-fourth Street, I saw Tom Jones as I headed toward Broadway. He was standing on the corner—not dressed for the weather. I stopped and asked what he was doing there. Tom said he was looking for the Apollo Theater. I, of course, had to tell him he was a "wee bit" downtown from the

Apollo. He said he wanted to see Chuck Jackson, who was appearing there, and I told him to get into the car and I would take him to Harlem to see Chuck.

We arrived backstage just before Chuck was to go on. I introduced Tom to Chuck, and Chuck brought Tom out onstage and introduced him to the audience. Now, you can imagine a "white guy" with a strange English accent being brought out on the stage of the Apollo. Chuck let the audience know that this was Tom Jones, the one who sang "It's Not Unusual," but the audience did not believe him. Most who had heard the song thought that the singer was an African American. Chuck asked Tom to sing just a couple of notes, and, of course, he blew the audience away.

I met Sonny and Cher in the '60s when we were all starting out. We did a television show together on a ship in New York and later did more television shows together. Chastity and my eldest son, David, went to the Tocoloma preschool together, so Cher and I became close friends as we met daily bringing the children to and from school. She's a bright and truly funny gal. It goes without saying she is talented and will be doing her thing for as long as she wants to.

Working early on in the UK as much as I did afforded me the pleasure of meeting and working with some of the brightest stars of that time. The Searchers, Dusty Springfield, Engelbert Humperdinck, Cliff Richard, and the Beatles—all are friends and, unfortunately, the losses of Dusty, John, and George were like losing members of my family. I am still in touch with "Enge" (as his friends refer to Engelbert), Ringo, Sir Paul, and Sir Richard.

I remember that while working at the Savoy Hotel in London in the '60s, I invited the Beatles to my show, and they said they would be there. When I came down from my room prior to the performance, I noticed there was a bit of confusion going on in the showroom. The Savoy showroom required men to wear a jacket and tie to be seated, and the room was full of very well dressed folks, some in tuxedos and gowns. As I peeked around the curtain to see what the ruckus was about, I saw my friends the Beatles being told they could not go into the showroom dressed as they were in jeans, sneakers, and T-shirts. They did have on jackets. With just about ten minutes to showtime, I made my way to the maître d' to let him know he had to seat my friends or I would not do the show. The surprised look on his face gave me the clue that he had never been told this before, and, without much argument, my four friends were seated (in very good seats, I might add) and the show went on. I had them come to my room after the show while I changed, then we all went to our favorite club, the Ad Lib, and had a wonderful time.

As a single woman, I could always spot a handsome man. Elvis Presley was one of the prettiest—yes, prettiest—men I had ever laid eyes on. Pictures and videos of him really didn't do him justice. I once told Elvis he was pretty, and he said, "How about handsome?" I said, "No, you're pretty." He fell out laughing. I will also add that he was one of the nicest men I ever met. The Sweet Inspirations, a singing group that included my aunt Cissy, two of the Gospelaires, Myrna and Sylvia, and Estelle Brown, were part of the background group that toured with him. He opened at the Las Vegas Hilton the same week I opened at the Sands. I went to the Hilton to see my aunt Cissy during their sound check. Elvis was there, and Cissy introduced me to him. He let me know he was a fan of my recordings, and this was a wonderful thing to hear. Elvis had all of the record stores place a photo of him inside of my albums (they weren't shrink-wrapped back in those days), and he announced from his stage that if his fans bought one of my albums, they would find an autographed photo of him inside of it. That week I think I sold more records in Las Vegas than I ever had. I will never forget this act of kindness.

I saw him several times after that in Los Angeles, where we were both living at the time. I was in the Marvin Hime jewelry store in Beverly Hills when he came in. It was during the Christmas holidays and, like me, he was looking for Christmas gifts. We started talking, and he asked if I knew of a good ear, nose, and throat doctor, as his daughter, Lisa Marie, had to have her tonsils removed, and he wanted the best to do this. I gave him the name of mine, who is the very best, Dr. Edward Kantor—yes, that is his real name (like the entertainer), and, yes, we all call him Eddie. Elvis took Lisa Marie to Dr. Kantor, who did the surgery, and she became a lifelong patient.

We lost an icon when Elvis made his transition. I smile when I hear some people think he may still be alive, and wonder what it would be like if he were.

I also wonder what it would be like if Karen Carpenter had lived. She and her brother, Richard, became friends of mine, and I remain friends with Richard. Collectively and individually, they are two of the most talented people I have known. When an artist or a producer decides to rerecord a song of yours, it is the highest compliment that can be given. When the newly recorded version has another sound, arrangement, and approach, making it that artist's own, it will get my nod.

Around 1970, I was invited into Herb Alpert's office at A&M Records to listen to the Carpenters' version of "Close to You," a song that I had recorded in the mid-'60s. I was pleasantly surprised. I loved the way Karen sounded. They also recorded a song I considered one of my biggest Bacharach challenges from the Broadway play Promises, Promises, titled "Knowing When to Leave." Karen nailed it.

It was such a pleasure to meet them, and I began going to some of their shows. Years later, in the latter part of 1982, I was staying in

New York at the Regency Hotel and ran into Karen. She was staying there, too. I hardly recognized her, though. She had gotten so very thin. I did not know at the time that she suffered with anorexia. It nearly broke my heart to see how frail she had gotten. I told her I would visit her in her suite the following afternoon, and I did. We had a lovely visit for about four hours. She shared with me that she was seeing a doctor in New York and was looking forward to beating the disease. I believed she would because of the conviction in her voice when she said it. In January 1983, I ran into her again in Los Angeles at a photo shoot for Grammy recipients. She walked up behind me and tapped me on my shoulder. She started laughing when she saw the look on my face. She had gained a bit of weight and even made the comment, "I have an ass again." We took the opportunity to catch up and laugh with each other. No one could have been happier for her than me. Her passing in February, a month later, shocked me and still weighs heavily on my heart. She was so young, only thirty-two years old, with so much to look forward to. I went to her funeral, which I am happy to say, reflected the fun side of her personality. Her friends were present and made sure the occasion was not marked by sadness. I do miss her, but her legacy is her music, and that will live on long after we are all gone.

I went to see Barbra Streisand at the International Hotel, which is now the Las Vegas Hilton, in 1969. I had seen her in *Funny Girl* and thought she was brilliant. But her actions onstage took away some of the positive perception and "glimmer" I had given her. As usual, her voice was impeccable; her designer outfit was definitely made specifically for her. But she was brash and sang mostly to the orchestra, with her back to the audience. Well, I was through. And no, I did not go backstage afterward.

While at Arista in the early '80s, I did go backstage many times to see the brilliant Bee Gees. I heard them for the first time on a recording that became one of my favorites, "How Can You Mend a Broken Heart." Their harmony is what caught my attention. I got a chance to work with Barry, Robin, and Maurice, and had a blast. They were easy in the studio and expected everyone else to be like them: prepared and professional. This included musicians, engineers, assistants, and most of all the artists they were working with—and in this case, that was me.

Clive Davis is the reason I got to work with "the brothers," as I referred to them. The story goes that Clive approached Barry at a dinner while visiting Florida and asked to meet him the next day to discuss the possibility of working with a few of his artists on Arista Records. When Clive asked Barry who on the roster would he like to produce, he said me. By this time the Bee Gees were one of the largest-selling recording groups in the world, with smash hits like "How Deep Is Your Love," "Stayin' Alive," "Jive Talkin'," and "Night Fever," to name a few, and I was excited. Barry and I met, and the brothers started writing and sending songs for me to listen to with the idea of making a record. I liked most of them, but the one I thought was just not me was "Heartbreaker." When Barry noticed that "Heartbreaker" was not on the list, he called and asked why. I told him I did not like it. He insisted that it could be a huge hit for me. We talked about it extensively in at least three or four different phone calls. He insisted that I record it, much as Hal had with "Do You Know the Way to San Jose." Since it was that important to him, I gave in. Again, needless to say, I was wrong, and he was right. "Heartbreaker" became one of my biggest international hits to date.

I also collaborated with my sisters. "Sisters in the Name of Love" was a show conceived by Gladys Knight in the mid-'80s. She called me one evening saying, "Sister, I need you to do this show with me," and I responded, "Where and when?" This is the relationship I have with Gladys; she is family. She also wanted Patti LaBelle on the show but was having trouble reaching her. She was trying to make contact by way of her management. I know from my own experience that inviting an artist to participate in a project by contacting the agent first can get crazy. Management can and do act as if *they* are the acts. I usually go directly to the artist and if they agree, they can let their management know. Gladys went through management and was told in no uncertain terms that Patti was not available to do the show. I asked Gladys why she had not called Patti personally. She said that she had asked where Patti, was to do just that, but was told Patti could not be reached. I then called Patti's husband, Armstead, to find out where Patti was, and he gave me the number of the hotel in Canada where she was staying. I called saying that Gladys really needed her to do this show. And because Patti is also a friend of Gladys's, she asked, "Where and when?" The show was a major award-winning hit. I look at it every now and then, and each time it is as fresh as the day we taped it.

Music industry icon Quincy Jones is another dear friend. I always said he reminded me of my doctor, who could have been his twin brother. Q, as he is affectionately known in the industry, has been applauded, and deservedly so, for his work in virtually every medium. He has worked with musicians and singers in almost every genre, garnered gold and platinum records, written and scored television and film, given back not only to the industry but generously to those in need on many occasions. And he gave his producing efforts toward the production and gathering of one of the biggest fund-raising recordings of our time, "We Are the World."

I got the call from him about "We Are the World" in 1985 while I was appearing at the Golden Nugget in Las Vegas. I wanted to participate but was obliged to fulfill my commitment there and couldn't be in LA at the time he needed me in the studio. Mogul Steve Wynn was the owner of the Golden Nugget at that time.

Q asked me to explain to him how important this project was and that I had to be there. I met with Steve and told him what was about to happen, and not only did he let me have that night off, he sent me to LA on his private jet.

The Who's Who of the music world was present for that recording. Some I knew and some I had the pleasure of meeting for the first time. The cause—to raise money to help end hunger in Africa—was great and the talent just as great; it was one of those evenings where, as is said, "You had to be there." The recording occurred the same evening as the American Music Awards, and it seemed that everyone who was at the awards ceremony showed up for the recording. I will not attempt to try to remember all of the names that were a part of this historic recording, but the ones that first come to my mind are: Stevie Wonder, Lionel Richie, Ray Charles, Cyndi Lauper, Diana Ross, Willie Nelson, and Michael Jackson (of course). The one thing I think all who gathered there will remember is the sign posted at the entrance of the studio: "Check Your Egos at the Door."

GET SOME of my best sleep on flights. A friend told me, "It's because you're sleeping with the angels." Planes are like a second home to me. And I stand in line and get checked just like everyone else.

My lifetime miles on Continental Airlines as of May 2010 were over 1,000,000, and my air miles on United Airways are over 488,000. And that, of course, I know only because of frequent flyer programs. Imagine all the travel time I logged in before. It's also from only two airlines. However, to put my air mileage in perspective, it's about 240,000 miles from the earth to the moon. Here's an entry from the journals I write in when I travel:

It's December 2009, and there are moments when I think I probably have more hours of flying than most pilots and flight attendants. I am now on my way to Tokyo, Japan, and will be spending my birthday 32,000 feet in the air. Japan is a place where I have had the pleasure of performing since the mid-'60s, and it happens to be one of the places that I look forward to coming to. This trip is a bit different for me, as I am not performing in concert halls like I usually do. This time I am doing the Blue Note nightclub.

When we landed in Japan, I checked my cell phone voicemail, and I had some wonderful birthday messages from friends and family members, including a message from Whitney. She sang "Happy Birthday" to me. It was a very special birthday, 32,000 feet in the air.

(Fast-forward, one week later.) We were in Tokyo for three nights, and it was wonderful. The shows were great, the audiences, as usual, were magic, and the folks at the club could not have treated us better. I had a chance to see some old friends that I've made over the years, and I'm sure my accountant will be pleased to know that I did not have time to do any shopping. (Bah, humbug!)

It was the first time that I stayed at the Hotel Okura, Tokyo, and I understand it is the same hotel President Obama stayed in on his visit here. My room overlooked the U.S. Embassy, and it really was a very pleasant stay. Tokyo, whose skyline is still bright, has grown to be a very fashion-forward city and is very expensive, as, I am told, are the other major cities in Japan. I didn't think there was a city more expensive than Moscow, but Tokyo is running neck and neck with it.

We went to Singapore and then on to Thailand, where I had not been in a few years. We landed in Singapore at 1 in the morning. It was 87 degrees, muggy as all get out, and promoters Ross Knudson and Lauretta Alabons were there to meet us. If you are in the business and are thinking of playing Singapore, you must work with Ross. He is the absolute best! The show was for the elite customers of Singapore Airlines and the airline's head honchos from around the world. We had a wonderful time, and I grew more proud each day of my son David, who travels with me and opens my shows. I must be honest: his stage presence and amazing vocal talent is making me truly earn my pay!

We left the next day for Thailand. I was able to get a good night's sleep and slept past 5 a.m.—Yea!—but not before some unexpected excitement broke out.

I have said many times to my group, stick with the "D" [me] if you want an adventure. Luggage call was 4 p.m. and, as usual, all bags were to be put into the hall outside of our rooms. Well, this was done, and as the luggage was loaded into the van, we all got into our respective vehicles to head for the airport. When we arrived at the airport, we had an hour and a half before we had to check in. It was at this time I noticed my bags were not unloaded from the van. Panic set in with Ross and Lauretta and, of course, with Deanna, my niece and road manager. Deanna is married to my brother Pookie's son, Barry Warrick.

Deanna swore she counted all 21 bags and couldn't imagine why my bags were missing. Cell phones came out and panic calls were made to the van and to the hotel. It appeared that my bags were never picked up from outside of my room, so Ross and I headed back to the hotel, since that was the only place they could be. Ross called the hotel from the car and was told the duty manager was on his way to the airport with my bags, so he had the car turn around to head back to the airport. Lauretta called Ross, her husband, and said he should go to the hotel just to be sure—and I'm glad he did because there sat my bags at the front door of the hotel. We loaded them into the car and headed back to the airport.

Needless to say, it was getting closer to boarding time. As we pulled up, the bags were rushed to the check-in counter, and, of course, it was too late to get both the bags and me on the flight, and, of course, they had given my seat away. So there I was without a seat and all of my bags. Inquiries were made as to the next flight to Bangkok, and we were told the three flights that could get me there in time to do my show the next morning were all sold out. So I spent another night in Singapore. Luckily, there was a flight out the next morning that got me to Bangkok. So, again, all's well that ends well! This was a close call, but by the grace of God, in the decades I've been traveling and performing around this entire world, I can't recall ever missing a performance. That's a record I'm very proud of.

DIONNE'S LESSONS LEARNED

- You can't judge a book by its cover.

CHAPTER 6

That's What Friends Are For

MOST PEOPLE who really know me know that *friendship* is an action word for me and an important part of what I am about. It's as vital to me as the blood that runs through my veins. I take neither the concept nor my friends for granted. I am lucky to have more than a handful of people who have always been there for me, as I have for them.

I'm sure that my friendship to some has been tested. You know, "Let's see if Dionne will do this for me" kind of stuff. I've had ample opportunity to do the same and have thought to myself, *Why should I have to test anyone to see if they are really in my corner?* So I've refrained from doing it.

In the early, dark days of the AIDS crisis, I saw firsthand the devastation caused by this deadly disease. The backstory to the recording session for the song "That's What Friends Are For" is an example of how friendship has worked for me.

One day in 1985, I ran into Elton John at the supermarket in

Los Angeles the day before the recording session. I asked him what he was doing in town. He said he was planning a birthday party for his then manager and would be around for a few days. I asked if he would be part of a recording I was doing, and I was met with an immediate yes.

When I called Gladys Knight, her only request was for me to pick her up, since she, like me, had just had foot surgery and couldn't drive. Since my surgery was on my left foot, driving was not a problem, and I told her I would.

Stevie Wonder was visiting his family in New Jersey when I called him. I asked when he would be back in Los Angeles, and he told me he was coming back the morning of the session. I asked if he thought he would be able to do the session that evening and he said yes, just give him the address of the studio.

Others who have always responded with a "yes," sometimes not knowing what they were saying yes to, include Nancy Wilson, Mary Wilson, Leslie Uggams, Senator Ted Kennedy, Senator John Conyers, Sammy Davis Jr., Frank Sinatra, Lena Horne, Prince Albert (yes, of Monaco), Berry Gordy, Clive Davis, Whitney Houston, and so many others from all walks of life. They all took that word *friend* as seriously as I do.

The recording session for "That's What Friends Are For" was done at Conway Recording Studios in Hollywood. And when everyone involved learned that the funds raised from this recording would go to amfAR, the American Foundation for AIDS Research, which Elizabeth Taylor cofounded, they signed on: We would donate whatever earnings we received from this project directly to amfAR. All fees were waived. That included the cost of studio time, the tape used to record, the video cameras, the engineer, videographer, publishing royalties of the writers—Burt Bacharach and Carole Bayer Sager—Arista Records, and the costs for the four of us: Stevie, Gladys, Elton, and me. We all gave up the royalties that we would have gotten and felt that if we saved a life, we would profit spiritually.

The evening was one to remember for the laughter and tears we shared making the record. I am and will always be proud of the fact that we were collectively able to sustain amfAR for its first two years of existence with the sales of that recording. Any funds garnered from the sale of this number one, Grammy-winning recording will go directly to amfAR in perpetuity.

The year after the release of the record, a major benefit concert was held at Radio City Music Hall in New York. It was called That's What Friends Are For and was hosted by Arista Records. The concert raised well over $2 million, which went to quite a few AIDS agencies in the fight against this deadly disease.

I also remember when, in 1988, I planned the first AIDS benefit that would be held in Washington, DC, at the Kennedy Center with what truly was a Who's Who appearing on the show. The event kicked off with a celebrity golf and tennis tournament. There were also educational workshops with health experts. Lena Horne and Blair Underwood hosted the evening, and Bob Hope hosted a celebrity golf day. The list of stars included the cast of the television series *21 Jump Street,* Luther Vandross, Nancy Wilson, Mary Wilson, Leslie Uggams, Exposé, Byron Allen, Barry Manilow, Howard Hewett, Holly Robinson, Burt Bacharach, George Kirby, Sugar Ray Leonard, Robert Townsend, Ted Kennedy, Clive Davis, Stevie Wonder, and Gladys Knight. Elton, whom I did not expect because he was in London doing the Nelson Mandela benefit show, was my surprise. He chartered a plane and flew to Washington to be a part of my benefit, making it the first time the four of us who had recorded "That's What Friends Are For" were onstage together. Yes, I emotionally lost it, shedding tears and more tears. Elton did something for me that was above and beyond the call. He will always be very dear to my heart. He is a rare personal friend and one who has remained true to our friendship.

The performances brought the house down. It was an electrifying experience for all of those who were in attendance. It was another one of those once-in-a-lifetime events where you just had to be there. "That's What Friends Are For" became a pop-culture phenomenon. And I'm proud to say more than twenty-five years later, "That's What Friends Are For" remains the anthem in the fight against AIDS.

It became extremely clear how desperately funding is needed for research, housing, and medical aid when I traveled throughout the world as U.S. ambassador of health and saw the devastation caused by this disease. Looking death in the face, which I did too frequently while on these trips, can never be an easy task. What became just as hard to do was getting people to understand the need for their assistance in this fight. I began to focus on educating people about the severity of this disease and the battle we all were in, as this disease does not care about race, color, creed, religious preference, or station in life. AIDS simply declares love of all, and I for one feel this is not the love anyone would want to experience.

Remembering those who lost their lives to this disease still makes me sad. To think of those with recognizable names, such as tennis great Arthur Ashe, a man of enormous talent who had his life taken in 1993 because of tainted blood containing the virus. And then there are so many within the entertainment industry who may not have recognizable names, such as the specialists in hair, makeup, lighting, set design, cameramen and camerawomen, engineers—the list goes on—not to mention the everyday hardworking people. It's still not easy to believe, nor should it be acceptable. I was shocked, as I know many throughout the world were, when, in 1991, basketball legend Ervin "Magic" Johnson let the world know he had contracted the virus and fast became a face for HIV/AIDS. He has raised the consciousness of all people and in so doing has done a great deal to rally people to give of themselves again to fight this disease. I still believe that we can win this war.

I have traveled, of course, as an entertainer, but I also traveled the world as the ambassador of health, giving and seeking information regarding the AIDS crisis. These particular travels took me to Asia, all parts of Africa, Japan, Malaysia, Thailand, China, and Europe, giving me an insight into the obstacles that I was about to face—mainly the denial that these countries were going through and the reluctance to face the reality of this deadly disease.

My appointment as ambassador of health came during the Reagan administration and lasted through Bush's term and the first year of the Clinton administration. And in all honesty, I saw more devastation than I ever believed possible. Death is something that I had never been confronted with, especially the magnitude that I was now seeing—babies, young girls and boys, the elderly—all because of a lack of knowledge about what they were facing and how to prevent it, the fear of acknowledging the problem, and the unavailability of medicines developed in the United States and Europe to other nations, too expensive to obtain.

I remember visiting a newly built state-of-the-art hospital in the Congo in central Africa that apparently was a place where patients with AIDS spent their last days. There was a lack of clean water to prepare formula for the babies, a lack of simple things such as cotton, beds, disposable needles, privacy screens, and bedpans. Upon my return to the United States, I made a request that the surplus that we have here be shipped to those regions I had just visited. However, to this day, I am not really sure if this was ever done.

During all my years as ambassador of health, all of my travel, lodging, and other expenses incurred were paid for out of my own personal pocket. I was offered full ambassadorship but turned it down. I guess you are scratching your heads, wondering why would I do that. Well, there's a very simple explanation: if I had taken the full ambassadorship, I would have lost the ability to go to the White House, Congress, and government agencies as a citizen to be the voice of the voiceless. Taking an appointment would have tied my hands in this way, because government rules and regulations prohibit someone who works for the government from making appeals of this type to the government. My movements and motives were monitored by the government, though. But that allowed me to find quite a few people in the system to align with the cause I was championing.

During President Reagan's second term, advocates for people with HIV/AIDS noticed and objected to the fact that whenever he spoke about this disease, he avoided saying the word *AIDS*. I never noticed until I watched some footage of him speaking at a function, and his talk included the "devastating disease" we were facing in our country and abroad. I thought it odd that he did not say what the disease was. President Reagan and I held a press conference announcing the work I had done and the progress being made, and it was during his comments that he again eluded saying the word *AIDS*. Then without any fanfare, I asked the president politely what disease he was referring to. With rosy cheeks and a bit of sweat appearing on his face, he finally said the word *AIDS*. I don't know if he feared coming down with AIDS if he said the word, but I am happy he found the courage to let people know that he could say "AIDS."

I stepped down as ambassador of health the first year of the Clinton administration because I just could no longer handle the amount of energy and work it demanded. I am, however, still very involved with trying to be of assistance in any way that I can. In 2004 I had the pleasure of hosting an HIV/AIDS fund-raiser in Germany with Bono, lead singer of U2. My involvement with the AIDS crisis was a personal mandate that I imposed upon myself. I made a promise that I would stay involved until a cure is found. And I will.

My grandfather, who was a minister, told me at a very early age he believed that we were put here for the purpose of being of service to one another, and he wanted me always to remember that. And to this very day, I do believe this to be true. The Bible I was taught from continues to give me the belief that we are all able to be of service to one another by just caring and giving of time, one of the most precious things one can give to another.

I come from a family of socially conscious people. So helping others comes naturally to me. Really, how difficult is it to give a dollar or two to feed twenty or thirty people? How difficult is it to give a coat, a dress, or a pair of shoes you no longer use to someone who can use them? I've been blessed, but whenever I encounter people in need, I say to myself, *There but for the grace of God go I.*

THERE JUST aren't enough pages in this book to express fully my passion for wanting to help people who have been affected by this disease. Unfortunately, HIV/AIDS and other devastating health issues seem to have taken a backseat in people's minds. The fires, mudslides, and earthquakes in Los Angeles, the floods in Manila, the earthquakes in India, and most recently the complete destruction of Haiti and the Gulf oil spill have overshadowed the ongoing fight against the pandemic. However, we can never lose sight of these public health issues that are faced daily by tens of millions all over the world.

DIONNE'S LESSONS LEARNED

- *We are put here for the purpose of being of service to one another.*

- *Caring and giving of time are the most precious things one can give another.*

- *There but for the grace of God go I.*

- *In battle, it's always primary to know what and whom you are fighting. Education is essential.*

My mommy.

That's my dad.

Me with Shaquille and Shaunie O'Neal: an amazing evening at the Muhammad Ali event, and meeting this couple was a highlight for me. (Getty Images)

Isaac and me at one of our "A Man and a Woman" shows.

My sons, David and Damon.

Leslie Uggams with her husband, Grahame Pratt.

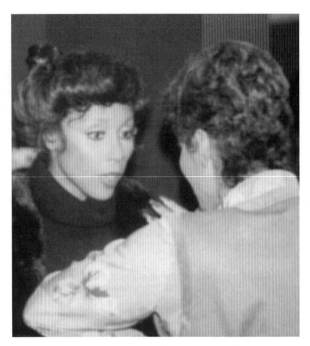

Talking with Diahann Carroll.

Sammy Davis Jr., me, and Frank Sinatra: my two mentors—here we go again, one more time. (Getty Images)

With my sons on Mother's Day.

Plácido and me . . . Christmas in Vienna.

Me and the Pope.

At the Grammy Awards with Quincy Jones, Michael Jackson, Stevie Wonder, and Lionel Richie: "We Are the World" Grammys—what a night! (Getty Images)

Me at the airport being checked; I guess I looked suspect! (Personal collection of David Freeman Wooley)

Barry and Deanna Warrick: "Ain't love grand."

Elton John, me, Gladys Knight, and Stevie Wonder—that's what friends are for.

My friend Elton John.

Bono and me: Bono works as tirelessly as I do regarding the continuing AIDS issue. (Getty Images)

Family affair: cousin Felicia, Whitney, niece Deanna, and nephew Barry.

We are family: Whitney, Aunt Cissy, and me. (Getty Images)

With Whitney during the World Women's Award ceremony in 2004 in Hamburg, Germany: a wonderful evening to be able to share with her as we both accepted a World Artist Award for Lifetime Achievement, the first given to women! (Jochen Luebke/AFP/Getty Images)

Onstage with Johnny Mathis: John and I had a ball touring this show; at that time, we held the record for attendance at Radio City Music Hall. (Getty Images)

Gloria Estefan, Smokey Robinson, and me getting our parts.

Gloria Estefan and me.

Rehearsing with Olivia Newton-John.

With Gladys Knight, my "Sistah G": It was glorious singing with her. (Getty Images)

Melissa Manchester and me.

The Spinners and me rehearsing.

With my son Damon and granddaughter Kaelyn at the premiere
for the movie Fame. Damon wrote six tracks for the film.
(Getty Images)

Philip Michael Thomas: a fun date with "my buddy" PMT. (Getty Images)

My duet partner, my son David Elliott, and me in action.

CHAPTER 7

The Torch

O N AUGUST 8, 1963, our family celebrated another birth— a little girl born to my uncle and aunt, John and Cissy Houston. They named her Whitney.

Not all infants are the cutest (as most people say when they see them for the first time), but in all honesty, Whitney was the prettiest newborn child that I had ever seen. I know you are saying, "Of course, she's related to you." But believe me, if it were not true I would not say it. I was, as was my entire family, so happy for Cissy and John—as well as Gary and Michael, Whitney's brothers—that another girl had been born this year. My aunt Annie had given birth in January to another beautiful girl, Felicia Anne Moss. The goal of having a little girl had once eluded me. Well, now I had two.

Everywhere I traveled throughout the world, I was busy in children's clothing stores stocking up on frilly, girly clothes for them both. It was a lot of fun for me to watch both of these little girls grow. Felicia was the quiet one, while Whitney was into everything.

I loved being asked to babysit them and found myself always looking for Whitney as she had, and still has, a wandering spirit and loved to hide from me. When I'd find her hiding place, she would jump out and say, "Peekaboo!" They brought plenty of laughter to our home. Both girls were baptized at the New Hope Baptist Church, our family church, and as they grew into teenagers, they became members of the church's junior choir. We gave them nicknames. Felicia was called "Filee," and Whitney was called "Nippy."

Being born into a singing family, it was predestined that they would be able to sing. So I was not surprised when I heard Nippy sing for the first time. She was twelve, and it was in church. She had a lead vocal on a song sung by the choir. Her voice was strong and full of conviction—much like her mother's—and she showed not an ounce of nerves. We took the children of my band members and background singers, including my aunt Cissy, with us during the summer months. So Felicia and Whitney joined my sons and the rest of the children on the road. There were at least eight youngsters, ranging in age from four to nine. It was always an adventure. A few hotels would not invite me back because, as we all know, kids will be kids.

In the several years that passed, and the kids began to age, the group got smaller and was down to six: Whitney, my two youngsters, my nephew Barry, Eunice Peterson's son Charlie, and recording artist Darlene Love's son, Jason. At ages six to twelve, they were a handful. They were introduced to riding in limousines, hotels with twenty-four-hour room service, and I will take the blame for teaching them how to use the phone to order room service.

I once left Barry, who was the oldest, in charge of the kids while I was doing a show in Las Vegas. Before leaving to go down to the showroom, I had ordered their dinner, which was sent to the suite. The kids asked if they could order dessert once they finished dinner, and I said yes. Ten deliveries of ice cream were brought to the suite. Needless to say, not only were there a lot of stomachaches, but the bill from the ice cream alone was more than I could have imagined: a whopping $1,380. This almost became the end of the "traveling kids brigade." But as they all grew into their teenage years, each of them began to have other interests, and traveling during the summers with "grown-ups" was no longer appealing. Every now and then as they got older, one or two of them would want to come out on the road with me.

Nippy remains very inquisitive. I guess growing up in a household with two brothers had a lot to do with it. She learned how to play basketball and baseball, and could run like the wind. And in the same breath, she was always very girly. She loved pretty things, clothes that had beading or anything that sparkled on them, anything soft to the touch, like velvet or cashmere, skirts, dolls.

She was around me so much I thought of her as "the little girl I never had," and that holds true to this very day. Nippy was a typical teenager; she loved being with her friends, going to the movies, and meeting at the local ice cream parlor. She was an excellent student and went to a Catholic school.

When she turned sixteen, she was discovered and began modeling for *Seventeen* magazine, traveling within the States as well as overseas doing photo shoots. I guess this was early preparation for what she is doing now. I was touring during her early teen years for months at a time. I was not around to know much about the boyfriend stage of her life. But I am sure she had her share of crushes and that one special young man. She didn't have much spare time because of the modeling. So learning to play cards or games was not a part of her growing years.

Holidays and birthdays were the special family times. Thanksgiving was the true family time when everyone would gather at my mommy's house, and she along with my Aunt Rebie would do the cooking. The menu would typically be turkey with corn bread dressing, glazed ham, string beans, mashed potatoes, yams, macaroni and cheese, sweet potato pie, and a four-layer coconut cake for me. Yes, my mother would make the cake for me, and nobody could have a piece until I said so. I did make them suffer. After dinner, we would go into the music room. I still don't know how we could stand, much less sing, after eating all of that food. But we did. Larry Drinkard, Aunt Rebie, Aunt Annie, Cissy, my mommy, and all of the kids, and my Uncle Nick would sit at the piano, and we would all sing gospel together. Any guest that joined us would be blown away being around all of those glorious voices. The looks on their faces said it all: they had been let in on the most wonderful secret. We would each take turns doing solos, and that included Nippy and the other youngsters, too.

When Nippy and Felicia were around eighteen years old, they developed interests other than singing with the family on Thanksgiving. They made plans to meet friends and asked if I would get them out of the house when the time came for everyone to head to the music room. And I did. I might add that I "caught it" from other family members for doing that. But hey, I was eighteen once, and I knew they wanted to be with their peers. I know what it's like to feel obliged to sing even if you don't want to. I know they both felt that way at times. I know I did. This was our ritual at Christmas, too. These special days at my mommy's house became a tradition.

The only time we all got together outside of our house was on birthdays. We went to the home of whoever was having a birthday to celebrate. I remember John, Whitney's father, would sit and listen wide-eyed and with the biggest grin on his face during those times when everyone was singing. He was a tall, very handsome man who had been welcomed into the family with open hearts. He joined our church and became very active in it.

My mommy and aunts and uncles used to travel the East Coast doing gospel programs in churches and concert halls. John would drive a few in his car, and my uncle Sonny and my daddy also drove to get the Drinkard Singers to their destinations. John was a good father. When he was not working driving long-distance trailer trucks, he always had time to spend with his kids. In the beginning of Nippy's career, he was on the road with her, and when her mother could, she would also go out on the road with Nippy, very much like my parents did with me. This gave her a sense of security and comfort. I know it made me feel safe and at ease to have my parents out with me.

During her teen years, Nippy and her brothers would come to my shows, especially when I would be appearing in Atlantic City. I think the façade of "glamour" caught her eye, and she was also being given exposure working with her mom, so I suppose it was predestined she would be bitten by the showbiz bug!

C ISSY LEFT the Sweet Inspirations to pursue her own career. It was during this time that Whitney was beginning to show promise of being able to sing on her own, and she started doing background sessions with her mother on recordings. Cissy would take her and her brother Gary to her performances to do background for her, and she started featuring Whitney doing duets with her on her shows.

Nippy performed with her mom at a small dinner club called Sweetwater's, located on the Upper West Side of Manhattan. It was a popular place, classy and intimate, holding around one hundred

fifty people. And it was there that she was discovered by a promotion man, Chris Jones, who worked at Arista Records. He told the
head of Arista, Clive Davis, that Whitney had a "gold mine" voice
like none he had ever heard. The following evening, Clive showed
up at Sweetwater's and was blown away by her sound and presence
at such a young age. Clive wanted to sign her right away, but Cissy—
like my mom had done to Burt and Hal in my case—said no. Nippy
was still in school, and her parents wanted nothing to interfere with
her education. Arista Records was not the only recording company
that had shown interest in Whitney, so the family had a lot to think
about where their daughter and a career were concerned. Cissy did
promise Clive that she would consider letting him have the first
chance at making an offer, but only when the time was right. The
right time was the year after Nippy's graduation from high school.

Whitney signed with Arista, and Clive took great care in preparing her for the world. The choice of songs, producers, arrangers,
photographers, stylist, hair, makeup artists—the whole nine yards
was carefully mapped out. He gave Whitney the very best, to our
families' delight. It pleased me no end to see the attention that was
being given to "my little girl"! She recorded a beautiful duet with
Teddy Pendergrass titled "Hold Me," released in 1984. The song
got some exposure with radio play and caught the attention of those
within the industry. Everyone wanted to know who this Whitney
Houston was, singing with Teddy. They soon found out.

Her first solo album, *Whitney Houston,* hit the record stores and
the radio airwaves in 1985, producing her first hit, "Saving All My
Love for You," which went onto the charts at number one. What followed were two more number one hits from the album: "How Will
I Know" and the ever-beautiful "The Greatest Love of All." She was
on a definite roll, and it hasn't stopped. Her videos were being seen
on MTV, a cable music network that was "mainstream." Whitney

was becoming, I'm sure without her knowledge, a pioneer within the industry.

Whitney was nominated for a Grammy with her first recording, and it just so happened that I was asked to present the Best Pop Vocal Performance, Female Award, one that I had won many years ago. I don't think anyone except me thought she would win. When the time came to open the envelope, her name seemed to jump off the card, and I screamed her name. Pierre Cossette, who produced the show, told me later that evening that the hug between Whitney and me was by far the longest hug in television history. I was extremely proud of her, and that night will live on in my memory forever.

Whitney's career continued to skyrocket as she was recording material that was suited for the time we were living in, and she was singing better than ever. More Grammy Awards followed, as did American Music Awards and BET Awards. She opened the path for quite a few more young African American female singers, and then film offers started coming in. A "little" movie titled *The Bodyguard* brought her prominence in the film world. Working with Kevin Costner had to be wonderful, and she always said that he was very generous. He told her that he would protect her, and when you watch the film, you can see he obviously kept his word. She was wonderful in her role, not to mention the kazillion albums of the sound track she sold worldwide. I know Dolly Parton had to be jumping up and down, since she wrote one of Whitney's biggest hits, "I Will Always Love You." Yep, this young lady was breaking all types of recording industry records, and now she was a big success in film. And she did it while she was pregnant with her daughter, Bobbi Kris, during filming.

She continued to act. *Waiting to Exhale* was followed by *The Preacher's Wife*. She was thrilled to work with African American actors of note such as Denzel Washington, Courtney B. Vance, Jenifer Lewis, Loretta Devine, and Gregory Hines. She was successful and having fun. She started becoming more involved on the other side of the camera by producing, too. Her first venture as executive producer was *Cinderella* starring Brandy, and her next was as producer of *The Princess Diaries*. The 1990s were becoming her banner years. I was at Super Bowl XXV in 1991 when she reinvented "The Star-Spangled Banner." The expression "She could probably sing the telephone book and make it a hit" applies to Whitney. After all, how many do you know who could record "The Star-Spangled Banner" and sell over a million copies? Well, she did.

To sell close to 200 million recordings worldwide is a feat yet to be matched by another female, and to say pride swells within me and our entire family is an understatement.

Whitney continues our family tradition of reaching back, too. She started a foundation and each Christmas would give loads of toys, food, and clothing to those in need in New Jersey; she has done many charitable events throughout the world.

Because of her meteoric rise to superstardom, I felt the need to talk to her about the kind of strength she would need to cope with how her life would change. I reminded her that she was not only representing herself but also her family, who would always give her our support and love. We would be the people who would have her back through thick and thin as she continued on her brilliant path.

But when she ran into a few brick walls, she learned that she was not made of iron, and that she was as fragile as the next human being. This was especially true in moments where, for example, Whitney would be hounded by paparazzi and have stories about her plastered on the covers of the "rags."

She was tested when she married Bobby Brown, as we all know. The marriage seemed to be working out at first and probably would have continued to if other people's opinions had not affected them. My involvement in her marriage was nil. Anything that went on within this marriage, neither I nor anyone else was privy to. She went through a very public divorce and dealt with the effects it had on her daughter. I empathize with not only Whitney but also anyone in the public eye who has to contend with private matters being exposed and criticized by anybody and everybody.

I will acknowledge that being a celebrity—and the loss of privacy that comes with being one—is much harder today than it was during the early stages of my career. With the advent of the Internet and the digital revolution, photos and videos can be posted online and viewed around the entire world within seconds of being taken. I didn't have to deal with all that. Nor were there paparazzi like there are now. In those days, most writers and journalists were respectful of when you were "working" and when you were not. Nevertheless, as celebrities, we all have to cope with some kind of invasion of our privacy, and it's not easy. However, it's part of the job.

Nippy got involved with things that were never a part of the lifestyle she was brought up in. But she ultimately came to the realization that she was doing harm to herself. She also knows the words and worth of prayer and has used it to bring her through all of the trials and tribulations put before her. That's why she continues to pass the tests of life with an A+.

The media exaggerate the stories they publish. Whitney, like so many of us, finds it hard to be deprived of the few moments that we can truly call our own. But again, as I have said, this is the life we have chosen.

I always treat celebrity "gossip" as an attempt to try to get a reaction from you, and recommend that anyone who finds himself or herself a target of such press not dignify it with a response. Make sure they spell your name correctly and always take the high road.

Whitney has been and will continue to be who she is, and that is a loving, giving, caring, and sharing person.

Whitney is enjoying the fruits of her labor again. She is an excellent mother. Bobbi Kris absolutely adores her and travels with her. She is again happy with herself, and it shows.

I was so pleased to have been home and able to attend the listening party of her new CD, *I Look to You.* It has already sold well over 2 million copies and is still selling. Her talent speaks for itself, and it makes me so happy to know her true supporters have kept her in their prayers. Her fans are once again attending her shows. I remember Whitney asking me, "How can you stay in this business as long as you have and not go completely crazy?" I reminded her that I *am* crazy, so there was no fear of the business making me that way.

Whitney is like the phoenix that rose from the ashes: bigger, brighter, stronger, and better than ever. This was evidenced when she did the two-part interview with Oprah Winfrey in 2009. She took each question and answered with truth, something a lot of people cannot or will not do. She looked gorgeous and made not only her family proud of her, but she made herself proud.

Oprah said it was one of the best interviews that she had done. Watching Whitney sing about not knowing her strength and hearing the conviction in her voice let me know without a doubt that she was again in complete control. Watching Oprah shed tears during her performance also let me know she was reaching into the souls of the audience, letting them know just how strong she is. She heard the words her mother and I both said to her: she "was not brought up to break."

Watching Nippy accept the Entertainer of the Year Award during the televised BET Honors in 2010 was also thrilling. To see the joy she felt as those magnificent voices serenaded her; the tears of pride shed by her mother and, I admit, me; the genuine joy being sent to her from the audience; the composure she showed with her acceptance speech letting all in that auditorium that evening and those watching at home know how wonderful it was not to be judged and how happy she was to be honored by her own!

I believe if the question "Who do you pass the torch to?" could be put to the late Sammy Davis Jr., he would have said Michael Jackson, and Michael would have said Usher and Justin Timberlake. Now within the entertainment industry, I believe the torch from Sarah Vaughan, Ella Fitzgerald, Marlene Dietrich, and Lena Horne (my mentors) was passed on to me. At this point in my life, it is without a doubt that I will be passing the torch to Whitney. This thing called stardom is a heavy wand to carry, since it requires total dedication to one's craft, and I believe her shoulders have broadened enough to be able to carry it with confidence and grace.

Whitney knows she will be carrying the torch and represents her entire family with strength, pride, and blessed humbleness. And one day, Whitney will be passing the torch on to Bobbi Kris, who has a wonderful voice; with her priorities in place, Whitney deserves the glory and praise being given to her.

She has earned it.

CHAPTER 8

Duet Queen

Even though I'd been recording for more than twenty years, for the first time in my life, I clearly remember feeling very nervous while listening to a track before going into the studio to record. And it was all because I was going to be recording with someone whom I absolutely idolized: the great Johnny Mathis.

When the producers finally asked if we were ready to make some music, we proceeded to go into the recording booth with our microphones facing each other. I was looking directly into John's eyes. By now, my nerves were really flaring, so much so that when I was to start singing, I was so mesmerized that I forgot to come in.

After everybody stopped laughing at me, I pulled it together, and we made a beautiful record. John was very kind to me and said he was flattered more than amused about my faux pas.

The song we recorded in 1982 is titled "Friends in Love." It was the first of two duets we did; the other song was "I've Got You Where I Want You." The session was produced by Jay Graydon, along with

David Foster, who also produced Al Jarreau, George Benson, and one of my all-time favorite groups, Earth, Wind and Fire, to name just a few. John and I were both very happy to be produced by them.

By the mid-'80s, I had become known in the music industry as "the duet queen." I had done so many duets with amazing artists. I even performed one with my cousin Whitney, a beautiful song written by my son David and Terry Steele titled "Love Will Find a Way."

David and Terry have written beautiful songs, including "Here and Now" for Luther Vandross, which gave him his first Best R&B Vocal Performance, Male, Grammy Award. I wish more people knew that they are among the best composers of contemporary songs.

All the duets have been fun to do, and I attribute this to the fact that my duet partners are all my friends. Luther was especially good for me to work with. He could sing anything at any time and make it sound like the only song you would want to hear over and over again.

I recorded "How Many Times Can We Say Goodbye" with him. He gave a magnificent performance and brought out the best in me. He felt the only way to do it was if we were in the studio at the same time. I think that's the way it should always be done. But many duets are done with the partners recording their part separately and at different times. I believe this is the way the Frank Sinatra *Duets* albums were recorded.

Listening to "How Many Times Can We Say Goodbye" today, you can hear the emotion, because Luther and I were in the studio at the same time, sharing the same microphone. We had the chance to react to what each of us was singing and give to the listening ear the full impact of the song's lyric. We probably spent more time laughing and eating that day than we should have, but when it was time to get down to business, we did our jobs.

Another session that ended up being a fun-filled evening was the "Love Power" recording session with Jeffrey Osborne. Jeffrey is probably one of the nicest people in and out of the studio. He also has a powerful voice. The song was written and produced by Carole Bayer Sager and Burt Bacharach and was recorded in record time. Burt will tend to want a minimum of twelve takes. But he had to admit that after recording five takes, we had actually nailed the song on the second take, and so he called it a wrap.

It took us all of two hours, which was an absolute record when doing a session with Burt. "Love Power" reached number one on the *Billboard* Adult Contemporary chart in 1987. It's on an album titled *Reservations for Two*. And the title song included me doing a wonderful duet with Kashif. The album also featured me with Howard Hewett and two dear friends, Smokey Robinson and June Pointer.

It was an awesome feeling to have another hit, since it had been twenty-five years since my first, "Don't Make Me Over." Years later, I was equally excited when my son Damon produced an entire CD of me performing duets with all female friends, *My Friends and Me,* which was released in 2006. This was one of the best times I ever had doing a recording session. I spoke with Gloria Estefan about being one of the guests on the project. She immediately responded yes, but only if she could do her favorite recording of mine, "Walk On By." I told her this would be fine, since my plan was to let each singer choose the song she wanted to sing. Gloria is one of those ladies who are perfectionists. I love how she approached it. And I'm very proud of her performance. As fate would have it, I happened to be in New York doing some recording, and Cyndi Lauper was in the same building recording at the time. I went to the studio where she was working and asked her if she would be a part of the project and she said yes. I told her I was in the studio down the hall and after she finished what she was doing to come there. I started playing the tracks for her, and she immediately asked if I was doing "Message to Michael." As it happened, the next track to be played was that song. Cyndi and I have been friends for many years, and it was an easy thing for her to lay her voice on the track. She was happy to be a part of the CD, and I just lucked out that she was in the same place as me at the time. Show business is all about timing.

Mya is one of my new friends. She loved the idea and said she would like to record "Close to You." She did her thing, giving the song a new flavor. Kelis is another new friend; it was very easy working with her. I like her sound and youthful approach on "Raindrops Keep Falling on My Head."

It was a bit of a twist to ask country singer Reba McEntire to be a part of the project. Damon was flying back to Los Angeles from New York and happened to sit next to her husband. They started talking and each found out who the other was. Damon thought it would be a good idea to ask if Reba would consider being on this project. Her husband said that he would ask her and would let Damon know. It was just a couple of days later that we got her response, and I am happy that she wanted to be a part of the session. She chose "I Say a Little Prayer" and gave a wonderful performance. She has a very distinctive voice, and the song suited her well.

Another country legend who was a part of the project is Wynonna Judd. I heard her sing "Anyone Who Had a Heart" when she appeared on a tribute show to Burt, and when putting this CD together, I thought that I would ask if she would like to do this song with me. She agreed. Damon and I flew to Nashville and recorded her there. It's obvious that she loves the song because the vocal performance she gave is absolutely beautiful.

"Wishin' and Hopin'" was not a song that I would have thought anyone would choose, but Olivia Newton-John let me know it was one of her favorite recordings of mine and that it was what she wanted to do with me. She showed up at Damon's studio, and after she and I decided who would sing what, we knocked it out in short order. Damon let us both know with these words: "It's so easy when you're working with pros." My granddaughter Cheyenne Elliott was eleven years old at the time we recorded "Love Will Find a Way." She did a wonderful job, and I'm very proud of her. The song we recorded as a duet is also very special in that it was written by her father, my son David.

"The Windows of the World" was recorded utilizing the beautiful vocal talents of Angie Stone, Chante Moore, Deborah Cox, and Da Brat, a hip-hop rapper. I love their performance. "Then Came You" was recorded by Lisa Tucker, one of the contestants on *American Idol* and an adorable young lady. And I think she also did a wonderful job.

Working with the internationally renowned "Queen of Salsa," Ms. Celia Cruz, was a most joyful experience. She, in all of her regal stature, was so much fun in the studio and took "Do You Know the Way to San Jose" to another level, as only she could. This version is the definitive way the song should have been recorded and is now represented on this CD. Celia danced. She scatted. She noted the many places in the world that have a San Jose. She was just wonderful, and I now go on singing and performing this song with a great deal of joy.

Gladys Knight was an easy one to record. And I already knew the song that she would choose, as she used to say to me, "One of these days I am going to record this song." Well, she finally had a chance to sing her favorite song of mine, "I Know I'll Never Love This Way Again," and as is her way, she definitely "showed out" and owned the song.

She always seems to bring out something extra in my vocal performances. I love singing with her. Even Damon commented to her, "Auntie Gladys, you *sang* that song." Then he added, "And Mommy, you weren't too bad, either." Kids.

BACK IN the '90s, in between all those duets, somehow I found time to develop my television show, *Dionne and Friends,* in 1990. The show, of which I was executive producer, came on the heels of the last time I left *Solid Gold.* It was done with my friends and also introduced current talent that I had the opportunity to meet for the first time. The production had elements that allowed the audience in the studio and those watching on television a chance to get to know the guest in ways that were not readily known. For example, Johnny Mathis had written a cookbook and is an excellent chef; he was featured on the show. There was the Walk of Fame segment that highlighted African Americans who made a difference in many walks of life, not only show business. One of my featured guests was a young lady named "Penny" who was fifteen years old and lived in a not very nourishing part of Los Angeles but found a way to be of help to the younger children by holding classes teaching the fundamentals that they needed. She had a burning desire to finish high school and go on to Harvard to become an attorney. (I am so sad that in tracking her progress, the researcher put on this dropped the ball, and I lost contact with her. I do hope she was able to realize her dream, and I intend to try to find her.) I also performed with Barry White, Gladys Knight, Michael Bolton, BeBe and CeCe Winans, and many others. It was most exciting. The show also featured the talents of Melissa Manchester, Heavy D, the Spinners, Jermaine Jackson, the Commodores, Randy Crawford, George Duke, Salt-N-Pepa, Peter Allen, Miki Howard, Stephanie Mills, Freddie Jackson, Olivia Newton-John, Angela Winbush, Deniece Williams, and others. I sure was hopeful that the show would run for a while, but unfortunately, it did not. It is something that I might think about re-creating somewhere along the line. You never know.

Nevertheless, over the years, television and I have had a wonderful love affair. I have done several variety shows, some at the very beginning of my career. There were the Danny Kaye, Bob Hope, Red Skelton, Carol Burnett, and Danny Thomas shows, to name a few. In 2007 I even performed on *Dancing with the Stars*. No, I didn't dance. There were also quite a few game shows. I was nominated for an Emmy for the show *Women to Women,* won a People's Choice Award, and played *Celebrity Family Feud,* which our team won.

But it was my first appearance on the *Soul Train* show during the '70s that excited everyone in my neighborhood. It was like being on the cover of *Jet* magazine for the first time. *Soul Train* was the first African American show that showcased African American recording artists and featured a predominantly African American audience, who danced throughout the show. Over more than thirty years, Don Cornelius, the show's creator and host, helped so many African American artists by giving us the exposure we had been historically denied on television. A few years later, Don came to my home to discuss the possibility of producing an awards show for artists who were not being looked at or nominated for the Grammy. I thought this was a brilliant idea and jumped aboard immediately.

I, along with Luther Vandross, hosted the very first "Soul Train Music Awards" show, live and in living color. Don and I were sensitive to the lack of expectations, but we not only brought in a show to be proud of, we also did something that most of these award shows still have yet to do: we brought it in on time.

I hosted the second show alone, as Luther felt he had gained too much weight and did not want to be seen on television at that time. The third show was my last time hosting. Music trends had changed, and rap and hip-hop began to set the tone of popular culture. I knew that this was not my genre, so I bowed out. I believe, though, that if we had stuck to the original vision, we could have given the Grammy Awards a run for the money.

Another wonderful show I had the opportunity to work on in the '90s was called *Celebrate the Soul of American Music,* which I coproduced along with Don Jackson of Central City Productions. The concept of this show was to celebrate industry icons who had never been recognized or given the honor of being celebrated, especially by their own. I must thank Don for giving me credit as executive producer.

I also worked with him in the early '90s on the Stellar Awards, and it was the first time that I had the opportunity to meet Mary J. Blige. She was "rough" around the edges at the beginning of her career. But she was an important part of the new sounds that were defining rap and hip-hop. Why she had been asked to do this show, I don't know, because the Stellar Awards honors the gospel community. But there she was, showing up to rehearse in her fatigues and combat boots. When the dress rehearsal for cameras was about to begin, most artists brought out what they would be wearing to show the colors. Ms. Blige was still in fatigues and combat boots. I asked if she would bring out what she intended to wear on the show. In not such a ladylike way, she let me know that she had on what she was going to wear. I had to say that what she had on was not appropriate for the show. I told her I could send one of the stylists out to get her something. But, without missing a beat, she again let me know in no uncertain terms that she was wearing what she had on. I then said she would have to wear that somewhere else, because she was no longer on the show.

I ran into her again a few years later at the inaugural groundbreaking ceremony of the Magic Johnson Theatres in Harlem and I almost didn't recognize her. She was beautifully coiffed and dressed to the nines. She approached me and asked if I remembered her, and I said I did. She thanked me for opening her eyes to the reality of who she should be and now was. Watching her become someone to respect within her community of young entertainers has been great. She is now the epitome of positive imagery and high self-esteem. She has fought the battle with negativity and won the war. Thank you, Mary J. Blige, for being.

I LOVE THE movie industry and have enjoyed being a part of the Academy Awards show a few times. The first time I was invited to sing on the show was in the mid-'60s when the song "Alfie" was nominated. I sat behind Sidney Poitier and could hardly keep my composure, as to me he was the greatest thing since sliced Wonder Bread. Sitting among some of the other greatest actors in the world was awesome enough, but it did not hold a candle to the fact that I was sitting behind Sidney Poitier! I received a standing ovation that night, and yep, Mr. Poitier was standing, too. Unfortunately, "Alfie" lost the award to "Born Free." It was disappointing, but for me the aura that surrounded that day was and will always be fondly remembered.

I also acted in a film called *Rent-a-Cop* with Burt Reynolds and Liza Minnelli. I'd be surprised if many people realize that. If you blinked, you missed me. Nonetheless, I would love to act in film again. In the mid-'80s, I was given an opportunity to wear another type of hat in film. I was asked by Gene Wilder to be the music coordinator for *The Woman in Red*. Why me? Aside from my being a friend of his and of his wife, Gilda Radner, and their both professing to being fans of my music, I had no experience in this area of the business. He gave me confidence when he said, "I believe you can do this."

Knowing nothing about what was expected of me, I went around asking a few people I knew who had done this before. Gene invited me to view the film at a screening room at Orion Pictures, which was financing the film. He had placed music in the parts of the film that he wanted. The music he chose as a placeholder was that of Lionel Richie, giving me the impression that that's who he wanted. My assumption was wrong, but when I made the suggestion to Gene, he actually thought it was a good idea. I called Lionel to see if he would be interested; he said he was, but his touring schedule would not permit him. So I thought of one of our most prolific composers: Stevie Wonder.

I called Stevie and asked if he thought he'd like to do the music for the film. When he asked me if I really thought that he could do this, the biggest laugh came out of my mouth. Can you imagine Stevie Wonder asking if anyone thought that he could write great songs—whether it was for a film or not? After composing myself, I answered with a resounding yes. I proceeded to let Gene know I had asked Stevie, and a puzzled look came over his face. I, of course, understood why. I told Gene, "Look, I know Stevie is blind," and, I said jokingly, "but he's not as blind as you think he is." I reminded him that he had said to me "I believe you can do this." I believed that Stevie could do this. Stevie had composed music for a short film, *The Secret Life of Plants,* but this would be the real deal.

A screening of the film was arranged for Stevie and me on the lot of MGM. I sat in an aisle seat and Stevie sat next to me. The film started—still with Lionel's music in those strategic places. When the scene came where Kelly LeBrock stood over a street grate with her red dress blowing around that perfect body of hers, Stevie asked me what was going on. I told him what was happening, what she looked like, and what she was wearing. When Gene's character was falling in love, hiding outside of her bedroom on a ledge, the audience broke out in gales of laughter. Stevie absorbed all of this.

I was a bit nervous after the screening and wondered if I had given Stevie more than we could both chew. He and I sat in the screening room alone after the film was over and talked about how green we were in this process, but we also agreed this was our shot to do something great and we should take it. He was given a video to take with him, and we went on our way.

My telephone rang at three the next morning, and when I answered, there was a very excited Stevie on the other end. "Just listen," he said. He had written the title song, "The Woman in Red," links (short pieces of music) for action and comedic scenes, the melody for "Weakness," and the ever-wonderful "I Just Called to Say I Love You." I had been sound asleep when he called, but I was now wide awake and overjoyed. That afternoon I met him at his studio, where he came with the work complete. I could hardly wait to let Gene know and started setting up the recording sessions.

Time not being Stevie's strong suit, you can imagine my chagrin when he showed up for the first session ten hours late. After dismissing the orchestra, I sat in the studio waiting. Angry? For lack of a ladylike word to use at this time—yes, I guess you could say I was. When he showed up, I lit into him, letting him know how disappointed I was with his nonchalant attitude. I also let him know that time was money, that we had a budget, and that neither of us could afford this behavior from him. I also said something that I am a bit embarrassed to admit. I told him 2 o'clock p.m. means 2 o'clock p.m. and not 12 a.m., and that it was not dark outside to everybody. I also reminded him that Berry Gordy, owner of Stevie's label, Motown, did not want him to do this at all, and both of our careers were on the line. He of course was apologetic and promised it would not happen again, and it didn't.

We finally got down to business, and he put his vocals on the tracks. He went on a short tour, and in his absence, I put my vocals and backgrounds on the tracks that were written for me. Strings and horns were added. Stevie was leaving for a tour in England. The young man who had mixed Stevie's recordings and I had arranged to meet at the studio to get started mixing and mastering. Because we were two weeks ahead of schedule before having to turn the music in, I felt it would be an easy time finishing—until I was told when I reached the studio that Stevie had taken the tracks with him to London. Not only did I scream, but I also sat in a chair and cried like a newborn baby. Once I got myself together, we called Stevie in London. I asked why he had taken the tracks with him. He calmly replied that he was not satisfied with a couple of his vocals and wanted to redo them. He promised he would have the tracks back to the studio within the next couple of days, and he did. As a courtesy, I sent the score to Motown for Berry to listen to. He in turn let me know that he did not hear a hit and still felt it was a waste of time and money for Stevie to have done this. Now, Berry Gordy is someone I had met in the early '60s. He came into the recording industry like a giant. What a joy to see a young, energetic, brilliant-thinking man take that part of the industry by storm. The Berry Gordy I know is a man with a wonderful sense of humor, a humanitarian, and someone who thinks he can play pinochle. Most important is that he is a friend.

But in this particular case, he was a friend who stood alone in his opinion. Thank goodness, his was not the consensus of the world. The record was certified platinum and won an Academy Award. And "I Just Called to Say I Love You" became an anthem. I made the right choice, and I'm so very proud to have been instrumental in providing Stevie the chance to win his first Academy Award.

DIONNE'S LESSONS LEARNED

- *Show business is all about timing.*

CHAPTER 9

I'll Never Love This Way Again

M Y PET name for those magazines that deal with the lives of celebrities is the "Misinformation Chronicles." I have also called them the "funny papers" and the "what we heard" papers and magazines. What could be of so much interest to people about the goings-on in the private lives of others? That's why it's called personal, because that's what it is: personal.

Don't we all have enough going on in our individual lives to be concerned about? I guess not, because these publications make a ton of money for someone.

I dated a football player named Tim Brown for quite a while during the '60s. He played for the Philadelphia Eagles. It was a wonderful relationship. I met Timmy, as he was known by fans and friends, at a recording session. My background group was hired to sing on a recording date that featured him singing as a solo artist. I won't say anything about his singing ability, but I will say there was an instant attraction. Cute? Yes! Tall? Yes! And what a body! He asked me out, and I enthusiastically accepted.

Our friendship grew, and I began going to his games when the Eagles played in Philadelphia. He introduced me to his surrogate parents: Ernie, a wonderful, feisty woman, and Al, a quiet and gentle man. I enjoyed a lasting and rich relationship with them. I, in turn, introduced him to my parents, and they got along and developed a relationship, too. In fact, everybody thought we were destined to marry. But our parents became a bit too involved. We felt like we were being pushed to take on more than we could handle. Our respective schedules kept us busy and apart. So we put the brakes on the path to matrimony and continued to be friends. We still went out occasionally, but outside demands on our time kept us from seeing each other on a regular basis. Tim and I eventually married other people. He seemed to be happy with his new life as a husband and parent. I saw him shortly after his marriage, and he looked wonderful. He had retired from football and was mentoring young boys and helping them to find their way in life. I ran into him again in Los Angeles, where we both were living, shortly after he and his wife had divorced. I had also gone through my divorce, so we had a lot in common. I invited him to my birthday party; he accepted and I'm happy he did, as there were quite a few members of the Los Angeles Raiders football team there, giving him a comfort zone. My experience with him also gave me a true love of football. Although the Eagles are not my favorite team—the Raiders are—I have to thank Tim and the Eagles for making me a football fan.

The one I gave my heart to was the brilliant French musician and composer Sacha Distel. I have great admiration and respect for him. Sacha cowrote the wonderful jazz standard "The Good Life." He was very French, and a true gentleman. We met while doing a television show in London. I remember sitting in the auditorium portion of the studio watching him on a monitor and finding the attraction to that image overwhelming. He was so very, very handsome, and someone I felt I had to get to know better. It appeared that he wanted to meet me, too, and when we did meet, electricity passed between us. After the taping of the show, he invited me to join him and his friends, Claude Deffe, Catherine Deneuve, and her sister, for dinner and to see Lena Horne. After the show, we all ended up at the Ad Lib club, and from that time right to this very moment, he will remain the one who owned my heart. I owned his heart, too.

Another special man who was and is, like Sacha, easy on the eyes is Philip Michael Thomas. Seeing him for the first time in the film *Sparkle,* I, like so many other women, thought, *My goodness. How can a man be that gorgeous?* My makeup artist, Wynona Price, worked on the television show *Miami Vice,* which Philip had starred in. Since I had the "in," I asked her to introduce me to him, and she did. Little did I know that he was in a very serious relationship with a young lady who was also the mother of a few of his children. I found this out after our relationship had developed. He is single, after all (I said to myself). We became closer, and when I was asked to make a guest appearance on another television show Philip was doing at that time, I accepted the invitation and played the role of a fortune-teller, of all things. Philip was, and I hope still is, a kind and very talented man. The last time I spoke with him, he was teaching.

I dated Gianni Russo after being told that he was "unobtainable." I had just seen him in the film *The Godfather.* We met while doing a television show. During the dinner break, he and I talked; he let me know what a fan he was of my music, and I let him know I had just seen the film. I said that I really thought he was not such a nice person to have been able to play with such conviction the part of Carlo, Don Corleone's son-in-law who abuses the Don's daughter. He took that as a compliment, as actors are supposed to lose themselves and take on the persona of the character they are portraying. He asked if I would have dinner with him sometime, and I told him to call me. He did, and our friendship began to grow. He lived in Las Vegas, and I was still playing Las Vegas on a regular basis, so we saw quite a bit of each other. He came into Los Angeles frequently, and it became obvious to both of us that we were developing into a "love affair." I use that term because I soon found out that he was married and had a daughter. I would have (and should have) stopped our relationship, but because he was supposed to be the one no one had been able to "get," I found it to be the coup that the "little brown girl" got him.

As time went on, interesting discoveries developed. He and I shared the same birthday. He had entrepreneurial aspirations, as I did. He loved the sun, as I do. He was an extremely good cook and would prepare some wonderful meals for me. He wanted to do many things and had really big dreams, one of which came to fruition. He opened a restaurant in Las Vegas called State Street, and it fast became the "in" place to have a great meal and "to be seen." My travel schedule was one of the reasons for the demise of our relationship. He had lots of opportunity to see and be seen. It wasn't long before he was spending time with a new woman. They ultimately married and started a family. He didn't have the courage to tell me himself, but what's left to say. His loss. For whatever reason, despite the fact that we were both in Los Angeles at the time, I never ran into him.

Edgar Bronfman Jr. was someone that I was rumored to have dated. But Edgar was and will always be like one of my children. We were introduced by Gary Keyes, who coproduced with Edgar the television special I hosted in 1976 called "The Original Rompin', Stompin' Hot and Heavy, Cool and Groovy All-Star Jazz Show." At the time, Edgar was a young, energetic, aspiring songwriter. Later he would become the marketing genius of the Warner Music Group. I introduced him to his first wife, Sherry, while doing this show. I took him to his first music awards show, the American Music Awards. He gifted me with a song that he had written as a birthday present and continues to invite me to functions that he knows I would enjoy. I know Edgar respects and has a warm adoration for me as I do for him because he continues to show me this to this very day. He will always have a special place in my life.

A man and a woman can be close friends without being involved romantically or otherwise, as is the case with Burt, for example. Most of my closest friends happen to be men. I've been privy to most of Burt's relationships with some incredible women and also the births of his children. I have been and still am friendly with all of his wives.

RELATIONSHIPS CAN be complicated. And being single and successful can be a double-edged sword when you are female. I suppose that comes from how we are taught and, in most cases, what we see in most two-parent homes. The man of the house is usually the breadwinner and takes care of the woman of the house. Both of my parents worked outside the home and shared the responsibility of taking care of our family. In today's world, the roles that men and women play in each other's lives, as it relates to who's head of the family, is often defined by who makes the most money and who's paying most of the household bills. This is very strange to me. Money shouldn't define one's status in a relationship—love should. When I think of the vows made during a wedding ceremony or the vows a couple in a serious, committed relationship may make to each other, it should be a mutual exchange and a responsibility to take care of each other. But this world of ours has gotten so infected with the "me," "I," and "my" syndrome, it seems that we have lost sight of the meaning of "we," "you," and "our."

Look, I have enjoyed the company of a few men who have filled my need for companionship. I have enjoyed every man who became a part of my life. They will always be remembered with a great deal of warmth. And yes, I still enjoy getting "girlied up" and going out.

Dating while single parenting is not an easy thing to do. It requires lots of mutual understanding on the part of the two involved. My children always came first, and if this was not understood, there was no reason even to begin a discussion of dating, much less having a relationship. It was understood that my children would not awaken to an "early morning stranger." Ladies, independence is wonderful especially when it is hard earned, and you should never be intimidated or ashamed of being or becoming independent. But please be aware that the male of the species in most cases can and usually will view an independent woman a rival as opposed to a partner whose accomplishments make him proud.

So before thinking with your heart, use your brain and do a bit of investigating. Will you be put into a competitive situation by making a man feel unable to take care of you or your needs as the relationship escalates? If children are involved, are they comfortable with him? You both should be entitled to happiness. I've always said that as long as there is a smile on your face, cool. When the furrows begin to enter the picture (remember, they create wrinkles), it is time to rethink the situation and, if need be, move on.

Remember, your life is just that—yours. "Be Who You Be and Let Others Be Who They Be."

DIONNE'S LESSONS LEARNED

- *Children come first, adult relationships second.*

- *Share responsibility in a relationship.*

- *Don't let your children wake up to an "early morning stranger."*

- *In a relationship, don't lose sight of we, you, and ours.*

- *Mind your own business.*

Through the years.

My fiftieth birthday party.

My sixtieth birthday party.

Me and Hillary Clinton: "Surprise."

Dave Wooley and me at the White House (with President Bill
Clinton's portrait). (Personal collection of David Freeman Wooley)

Beverly Todd, Henry Carr, Winnie Mandela, and me.

Me and President Clinton. (Getty Images)

"My sisters": Gladys Knight and Patti LaBelle.

Arif Mardin and me at the Cole Porter recording session.

On Tavis Smiley's show, promoting my children's book, Say a Little Prayer, with Dave Wooley. (Personal collection of David Freeman Wooley)

Me and Mommy.

My granddaughter Cheyenne doing her thing at B.B. King's in New York City— she got a standing O.

Cheyenne: That's a big communion bubble!

Kaelyn with her daddy, Damon.

Damon and David.

Cheyenne and her daddy, David, her best protection.

Receiving my star on the Walk of Fame in Hollywood, with my sons, David and Damon, Dee Dee, and Mommy.

With Burt Bacharach and Hal David: the "triangle marriage" all receiving "rewards" from NARAS. (Getty Images)

Mommy presenting me an award for my thirty-fifth anniversary in show business.

That wonderful smile of Luther Vandross.

The Legends Ball: Legendary status came sooner than I expected. Thank you, Oprah!
(Getty Images)

While in Abu Dhabi: Hey, to me it was just like riding a horse—not!

My home in Brazil: If you look closely, you can see the Christ statue.

I love Christmas.

On the American Idol *season five finale, singing "That's What Friends Are For" with* American Idol *contestants. (Getty Images)*

Catching up with "Ree" (Aretha Franklin). (Personal collection of David Freeman Wooley)

Cheyenne, Dee Dee, and me: just being us.

Five of my six grands: Mya, Cheyenne, Kaelyn, Lealand, Mandela.

My grandson Neko.

Dee Dee, Mommy, and me.

Teddy Pendergrass aka "Theodore" (as I called him) with his new bride, Joan, and me at the R&B Foundation Awards show. (Personal collection of David Freeman Wooley)

Greeting one of Lena Horne's grandsons at her funeral service. (Getty Images)

Proud poppa David and proud Grammy with Cheyenne at B.B. King's in New York City.

CHAPTER 10

Age Is Just a Number

T HE FIRST time I thought aging was a problem, I had just turned thirty and was having dinner with my daddy. I said to him, "I'm getting old, and I don't think I like it." His response to me was, "Young lady, you thank God that He has allowed you to even say you're getting old." After giving this some thought, I realized he was absolutely right. I was blessed to have been able to open my eyes that morning, get out of bed without assistance, do all that got me prepared to face the world and with my right mind so that I could deal with whatever life brought me.

Celebrating my sixty-ninth birthday was joyous, even though I was 32,000 feet in the air on my way to Japan. Yep, I'm sixty-nine and counting. The old saying "Age is just another number" is so true. If what time represents are lessons learned, goals met, and good health, then you are ahead of the game of aging.

Beautiful women I have met over the years, such as Lena Horne, managed to stay ever young, giving me and all women hope of being

149

Daddy's girl: me and my daddy, Mancel L. Warrick.
(Personal collection of Dionne Warwick)

able to preserve their looks if they are willing to take care of their health. All else follows.

I can't honestly say that I have what others might refer to as a real health regime that I stick to. Most of the time, I don't eat a balanced meal. Nor do I drink tons of water or exercise a lot—unless walking through malls can be considered exercise. I simply don't do well with things that require a governed schedule. However, when I feel like it's time to drop a few pounds, like I do now, I will try to add a few more greens and a few V8 juices instead of my beloved Pepsis.

Over the years this has worked for me. Your body changes with age, but so does your mind—which happens to be the strongest part of your body. So my trick is to keep the gray matter pink. Use your brain more often and direct it to do what you feel needs to be done.

Once, I had an eight-hour dental surgery, because I was losing bone throughout my gum line. Bone was taken from my hip and infused into my gum line, giving me the "hippest mouth in town." That surgery prevented me from eating what I really wanted (steaks, ribs, corn on the cob) for two weeks. As a result, I lost fifteen pounds and looked incredible. Now, I am not suggesting you look at dental surgery as a way to lose weight, but it worked for me.

Skin care has been and will always be a concern of mine. I was fortunate in that both of my parents had great skin. But we all can use some help in this area, even with good genes. I also met Dr. Edgar Mitchell, who took great care of my skin for many years. When he was no longer able to do so, I found another brilliant doctor in Los Angeles whom I swear by. Her name is Dr. Veronica Lazarus, and she is truly the best. She created a skin care line for me that I am religious about using. It is called ENYO, which means "perfection." It's an easy process. The regimen is really basic: cleanse, hydrate, and moisturize the skin, and problems will never arise. When that pimple or blotch happens to show up, it can be easily handled by another product we added to the line, a serum specifically for eruptions. I feel strongly about cleanliness, because your face and body will let you down if you don't keep them squeaky clean.

I smoke and have smoked for quite some time. I am always getting from friends and people generally, "How can you smoke and sing?" And I answer by saying that smoking is what gives me my sound—although I know that's a crock. It just makes me feel better. We all know smoking is bad for your health, but I enjoy it. I will confess, though, that I have made the promise to myself that when it appears to be affecting the voice is when I will stop. And I don't smoke when I'm preparing to record.

I remember when both my sister and I thought we were old enough to start smoking and took two cigarettes from my mother's pack. We went into our bathroom, opened the window, and lit up. We blew the smoke out of the window, thinking we had this covered. Mommy came home from work and went into the bathroom. When she came out she asked us if Daddy, who also smoked, had just used the bathroom. We both said no. She then asked us to go into the bathroom and to let her know if we smelled cigarette smoke. We went into the bathroom and, oh boy, did we ever smell the smoke. Naturally, we wondered how that could be since we had blown the smoke out of the window. She gave us each a pack of her cigarettes, sat us down at the kitchen table, put ashtrays in front of each of us, and told us to light up. We, of course, thought this was wonderful: Mommy understood. Not. We lit the first one and after we finished it, she had us light another one and let us know that we would be smoking the entire pack of cigarettes. Needless to say, *sick* is nowhere near the word for how we felt after smoking twenty cigarettes in a row. I did not look at another cigarette until I started college. I began smoking again while typing my thesis in addition to the papers of eight of my classmates who'd asked me to type theirs, too.

I am extremely happy that neither of my sons ever had the desire to smoke and they both are constantly on me and will not allow me to smoke in their homes or their cars.

B EING A woman at any age who is fashion conscious can pose some unique challenges, such as finding the right beautician, or the right dresses and shoes, among many other needs.

My image has always been very important to me. Early on, I used to shop at a store called Elsie Sommers Boutique in South Orange, New Jersey. Elsie carried designer clothing and gowns. In the beginning of my career, most of my gowns were bought from her store, and it was there that I met her daughter-in-law, Valerie. We became very good friends and she began taking me to the showrooms of some of the designers whose clothing was carried in the store. Designers such as Oscar de la Renta, Bill Blass, Giorgio Sant'Angelo, and Valentino, just to name a few, became some of my favorites.

It didn't take long before they all started creating designs for me. At that time, I was doing quite a few variety-type television shows. It was during one of these shows that I met a young man named Michael Travis, who was head of wardrobe for most of these shows. He designed beautiful costumes for the shows, and I asked if he would design a couple of gowns for me. He did, and fast became my personal designer.

Michael created incredible looks for me. He was the creator of the ball gown with jeweled form-fitting belts for me. He was the innovator of the "fringe look." His fabrics were one of a kind, imported from Switzerland.

It was a joy to wear Michael's creations. They garnered many compliments from people who let me know that they would wait to see what I would be wearing either in concert or on television. Michael began getting calls from some of my peers and began designing for the O'Jays, the Fifth Dimension, and the Supremes. He also designed for Mitzi Gaynor, Ann-Margret, and many others. Unfortunately, Michael has multiple sclerosis and had to retire from designing.

My feet were also of primary concern regarding my comfort. The shoe designer that I swear by became my staple shoe of choice, Stuart Weitzman. This man had to have had a wife, daughter, or girlfriend who let him know that it was important that comfort be considered along with his creation of styles and the beauty of his shoes. And if he did not have this advice given by the above mentioned, then he was simply a flat-out genius. I'm forever grateful that he designed shoes that allowed me to move gracefully across a stage without pain.

While I lived in Los Angeles, I was introduced to fine jewelry by the Frances Klein antique jewelry store and Braun Brothers jewelers. When it came to jewels, they were my mentors. They gave me the most information regarding just how much I should be paying for certain pieces and what to look for regarding flaws. Frances Klein was very motherly to me. She told me that I had only five fingers on each hand, one neck, and two wrists, and I should think before I spent. She also said I should always keep in mind to buy what I needed—and only on occasion buy what I wanted. She was absolutely right, and her advice saved me bunches of money.

I remember while performing in St. Moritz, Switzerland, I met Harry Winston, the famous jeweler. He was there to do a jewelry showing and asked if I would like to wear some of his jewels while doing my show. Hesitation did not enter my space. My response was a very loud "yes." This was one of those gala events that the Who's Who of Anywhere attended.

I thought, well, I'll be wearing a lovely ring or bracelet of his and would be the stunner of the evening. An hour before I was to go down to do my show, Mr. Winston's courier came to my room with what I was to wear.

I nearly fainted when that man opened that pouch. He was carrying diamonds galore, a necklace, bracelet, and rings. And since I did not wear earrings at that time, they were the only things that I did not have on my body. I instantly became the $5 million lady.

I made the man stay with me until I went to the ballroom. I

didn't want to be attacked and robbed on my way to do my show. When I went on the stage, I thought I would pull rank. I looked out at all those very beautiful and famous people, and I let them know that they could call me "sparkle plenty." Then I asked the ladies in the room if they knew the jewelry designer I was wearing? I had a very smug face while doing this. Well, they took that smug look off my face immediately, when, like an ensemble, every woman in the room said loudly, "Harry Winston!" Each of them was also wearing his jewelry.

After the show, my valet Willie and I headed back to my room. We had planned to go to Chez Regine, the disco in the hotel. Willie and I sat and waited for the courier to come pick up the jewels, but after more than an hour of waiting, it was apparent this man was not coming. So we actually removed the mattress from my bed and hid the jewels under it. We went to the disco, only to see Mr. Winston's courier out on the dance floor doing all the latest moves. He was having a good time. And he did not seem to be concerned about the jewelry. I guess not; who in this room would think to steal these baubles? No one.

One of my other loves of fashion is my love of fur. This love of furs was inherited from seeing my mommy and my aunts wear them.

My furs were designed and made for me by a furrier in Las Vegas. Ray LeNobel and his wife, Anna, had a fur store in the Dunes Hotel. They have designed all of my fur coats for me, including my silver fox, red fox, mink, sable, and lynx.

I have been asked if I was afraid to wear my furs because of the folks who were throwing paint and other things at people wearing fur. This, I believe, is absolutely crazy. And I have a "message" to all these folks who are doing this: if you ever attempt to do this to me, you will personally meet "Ms. Crazy."

Moving on. As a very young lady, I used to practice walking like my mommy and all of my aunts. I attribute the way I carry myself to the women in my family who moved with ease and a very regal carriage. So if I have a "swagger," it comes from those wonderful ladies.

Who knew, many years later, this practicing to walk would be very helpful, as I have on several occasions walked down red carpets at the Grammy Awards, the Academy Awards, the NAACP Image Awards, the American Music Awards, and a few other award-type shows. These events can be fun. However, they can also be zoos. It comes with the territory.

Okay, now for—the hair.

In the beginning of my career, I wore a wig for about two weeks. It was the thing to do at the time, or so I thought. I felt it looked like a big old hat sitting on my head. It also made my head itch. Hey, I'm just trying to keep it real. I remember coming offstage after a performance and snatching that thing off my head. And it seemed like I just couldn't stop scratching my head. That was it. I stopped wearing wigs and started styling my own hair.

Later on, I was very lucky to find a young man named Clifford Peterson in Los Angeles who took care of my hair. He had the "hands." I've always believed it is the beautician's hands that give one's hair the total and special connection to your "crown." Without a doubt, he gave this to me.

Clifford took care of my hair, my "tresses," as he called it, up to just before he made his transition. It has been quite an adventure finding someone with the "hands" to take care of my hair.

This led me to try extensions. I have to say I made a costly—a couple of thousand dollars—mistake. The style was wonderful and it did keep me from putting heat (curling irons) on my hair for a few months, but the torture I went through. I still wonder, was it really worth it?

I sat for hours while this person braided my hair so tight that it made my naturally almond-shaped eyes take on the shape of cat eyes. And yes, it hurt! I looked like Catwoman with a face-lift. After the braiding was done, she then started applying the hair by sewing and attaching it to the braids. More pain; I don't believe I put my head on my pillow for more than a week because of the tightness and the pain I was experiencing. Yes, I was cute for a few months. But if that was what I would have to go through just to be cute, then I would simply have to give up being cute.

After a few weeks, this infused hair began making my scalp itch. I don't like having my scalp itch. So I methodically started removing each strand sewn into my hair. This was no fun.

I was on tour and couldn't get to the shop that had put the extensions in, so I had to do it myself. I learned from a beautician in one of the hotels where I was staying that if I bought some conditioner and drenched my hair with it, the braids would loosen and it would be much easier to dislodge the extensions. It was like a miracle. She was right, and it was done in a lot less time than it took to put those things in my hair. Now, for those who choose to wear wigs, weaves, extensions, or anything else—that's fine with me, because it's about your choice and/or your circumstances.

My search continued to find the "hands" for my hair. As luck would have it, I was doing a video shoot in New York. The person hired for the shoot was also hired to do my hair. He is a very sweet young man named Smitty. And he did a wonderful job on my hair. I had finally found the "hands" that I had been looking for. I'm elated to say Smitty is still making magic with my hair.

Keeping my hair clean and conditioned is very important to me, so I'm always looking for new and improved hair care products. However, with the number of hair products on the market, it's a wonder anyone could tell you which is the better one to use.

I have looked at the ingredients listed on several shampoos and conditioners, and have found 99 percent of them all contain the same ingredients. So I suppose it comes down to how many times you see a product advertised or if you have fallen in love with the name of the product. Because if they all have the same ingredients in them, then they must all be the same. As long as the result from the shampoo is clean hair, and the result from the conditioner is luster and softness to the hair, then I'm fine with the product.

Before leaving the subject of hair, here's just a little heads-up for the men: Never, and I mean never, just arbitrarily touch an African American woman's hair. Each woman will have her own reasons for this, and you risk losing your hearing—after being yelled at—or worse. Please, take this pearl of wisdom to heart and just Do Not Touch the Hair.

Also, who and what determines the terms "good hair" and "bad hair"? Ultimately, this has to be your decision. If hair holds a style, is kept clean, and is not abused too frequently by coloring, straightening, and hot irons, I would consider that "good hair." "Bad hair" is the result of those abusive treatments mentioned.

Yes, I color my hair. But I also will allow those "white peaks" to peek through because I know the chemical content in color can cause real damage. So instead of putting color in the minute I see those peaks, I will wait a couple of weeks before covering them. Besides, at my age, I earned every one of those peaks of white.

DIONNE'S LESSONS LEARNED

- *Age is just a number.*

- *Your mind is the strongest part of your body.*

CHAPTER 11

People I Admire

THROUGHOUT MY career, I have been very fortunate to have had some extraordinary people touch my life. These people have provided me with a multitude of positive impressions from which I have learned some valuable lessons. And in my own way, I have taken what I have learned and tried to use it for the good of others.

Oprah Winfrey is high on my list of most admired people. Her tenacity, high standards, and generosity are examples for us all. She does her homework and has complete control of the subject matter before speaking and/or taking action. Her true sense of giving back is well documented, and I for one have had the pleasure of being on the receiving end (I'll speak more on that later) of her decision to give back to those she felt gave her the "bits and pieces" that make her who she is.

There are not enough pages in this book to begin giving the lessons that I have learned and will continue to learn from Maya

Angelou. She is an incredible lady and truly a doctor in every aspect of the word. Dr. Angelou has the ability to teach, preach, and heal through her beautiful command of words. The wisdom she shares through her books, writings, and lectures give empowerment to all. And those who have read her books or attended one of her lectures have to walk away with the sense of "I can do that!" This is the message she has delivered to me, and I appreciate her for sharing it with me and the world.

A woman who along with her husband helped change the world is Coretta Scott King. She was a woman of so many qualities of faith and courage. Her belief in freedom and education, especially for those who "looked like her," was a brave stance she took and believed to be her calling. Although she spoke softly, she wielded a very big stick. Her passion for women to excel in everything the world had to offer was as wide and broad as the world we live in. She walked the talk and exemplified the dignity that she felt was to be given to all women.

Someone who also has dignity and that real "girlfriend" quality is Hillary Clinton. When I met her, I felt that I had known her all of my life. From our first hello, she was so down to earth and has remained that approachable person to this very day. This is the one quality that those who have attained a certain highly respected station in life could all learn from. Being married to the president of the United States is in itself probably the most daunting spotlight that anyone could be under, with every move, word, look, and style being scrutinized by the entire world. She handled it, even when she came under criticism for using "um" during a speaking engagement. Silly things like that. But she stood tall and has always had the ability to brush that kind of silliness from her shoulders and keep steppin'. Now, we all know the pressure she is under being secretary of state and what she is accountable for. In my opinion (which I do respect)

Hillary is doing a magnificent job and is making me proud to say, "I know her personally."

During one of my several visits to Washington, D.C., I was introduced by Congresswoman Yvonne Brathwaite Burke to an incredible lady, Barbara Jordan. Ms. Jordan's righteous spirit filled any room she entered. Her power was in her incredible ability to speak with apparent ease to issues that concern us all. The way she enunciated each word, making certain that she was totally understood, made her the orator of orators. I had the pleasure of being in her company and performing for her when she was honored by the state of Texas. I asked her if she would allow me to look into the possibility of having her life story written and presented as a theatrical piece. She felt, in her words, "I have not finished living, so wait until the time has come, and it will be my pleasure to permit you to do this." I let her know that if there was ever a person who could make me consider giving up my singing career to become an attorney, it would be her. Who can forget the keynote speech at the Democratic National Convention in 1976 or the call in 1974 for the impeachment of President Nixon? I know I won't.

I am very much involved at this time lobbying for a U.S. postal stamp with her image, and I am hopeful my endeavors to obtain this deserved honor for her will be accomplished soon.

There have also been several men who have made indelible impressions on me from which I have learned as well.

There are no words that suffice to describe how I feel in the presence of Nelson Mandela. It is my greatest honor to be one of his ambassadors for his foundation 46664 (Mandela's prisoner number), and I was installed by Mandela himself during the AIDS International Conference in Asia more than ten years ago. At the age of ninety-one "Madiba," as he is affectionately referred to, is truly a man for all seasons.

When you can go from being a prisoner for twenty-six years, living in a "cubby hole" in South Africa, to become president of the very same country—says it all! You want to leave a room walking out backward with a bowed head once you've encountered him. He speaks to all mankind. His mantra to "listen to and to speak to" is one that we can take a long, hard look at making our own practice.

Another wonderful man who became a president is Bill Clinton, who, like his wife, is a very easy person to know. Again, I felt he was someone I have known for a very long time, a friend, and he continues to present himself to me in exactly that way.

I became aware of him while watching C-SPAN late one night. He was governor of Arkansas at that time and was speaking about the wonderful progressive things that were happening in "his" state. While he was speaking, I felt as if what he was saying could and should be applied to the needs of the entire United States. I was impressed, and I started asking friends and those I knew in government whether they knew anything about him. Not many did, and I decided to find out more.

My road manager at that time was Jack Nance, who was from Arkansas. I thought Jack might know something about Bill Clinton, so I asked if he knew him. Jack said that he played golf with his brother. I told Jack about the C-SPAN speech and how I really thought he would make a great president. I asked if he would get a contact person or number for me. Jack provided me with the phone number to his office and I called. He was not available at the time I called, so I left a message asking if he would return my call.

To my surprise, Governor Clinton did return my call, but unfortunately, I was out of town. We played telephone tag for a couple of weeks and finally connected with each other. I let him know how impressed I was with his talk on C-SPAN and asked if he had considered running for president because I felt all that he spoke about was what the entire United States needed to hear and feel could be accomplished.

I know he must have thought I was crazy, but he was polite enough to listen to me, and I let him know that I was going to start a write-in campaign to help persuade him to toss his hat into the presidential race, and I did. As time progressed, we are all witness to what transpired. I along with these United States saw the benefit of electing him into office. His work continues with his tireless efforts to make the world a healthier, better place for all.

I have also been inspired by another man who has made a major contribution to our country, General Colin Powell. The general is a man of accomplishment and stature to be reckoned with. He is a very personable man who obviously loves his country, as he put his life on the line for it and for us. Meeting him was a complete honor and a true treat. He is a family man, with the humility to say "I'm sorry" and to admit when he is wrong.

I performed at his request for his wife Alma's organization, the National Council of the Best Friends Foundation, which helps young ladies find themselves, improve their self-esteem, and be empowered to attain goals they may have thought unattainable.

Okay, now it's time to talk about a man who's tall, dark, and oh so very handsome: Mr. Sidney Poitier. He's a complete gentleman, one that I know to be completely dedicated to his family, his ambassadorship, and his craft. When, in 1963, he became the first African American man to win the Academy Award for Best Actor, I was too young to really know the significance of what it meant in the world of acting and in our world generally. To be "first" is a heavy burden in most cases, but in Mr. Poitier's case it was a first well deserved, and he wore it with dignity and pride.

I remember as a teenager actually following him in New York City one afternoon. Yep, just like a stalker. We had just finished a demo recording session and as we were walking down Broadway, I spotted him and completely lost my mind. I proceeded to follow him for a few blocks to say hello. My sister, Dee Dee, said I was crazy—and I probably was—but this was *Sidney Poitier* in the flesh and I had to say something.

I was totally embarrassed when he finally turned around and politely asked, "Can I help you, young lady?"

I was too flustered to speak. He looked me in the eye and said, "Please say something." And that is what I said: "Something." He let out a hearty laugh and gave me a hug and went his merry way.

Sidney has reminded me of that many times.

All of the honors that he has received so far—including the President's Medal of Freedom presented to him by President Obama—are, to me, just the tip of the iceberg of honors he should receive.

Our president has also made an indelible positive impression on my life. I first had the pleasure of meeting Barack Obama during his first year as a senator from Illinois. He's personable, an exceptional orator, bright, witty, and one who deserves to be the leader of these United States. I campaigned vigorously for him when he ran for president.

I attended a political rally in 2006 in my hometown, East Orange, and at my old high school, just a few blocks away from my home. Three hundred folks filled the auditorium to overflowing. He began by giving recognition to all the political dignitaries seated on the stage, and as he spoke, he looked right at me and paused. I must say, this came as a complete surprise when Senator Obama said, "Dionne Warwick is in the house."

He went on to say how my music had played a very big part in his life. And he proceeded to let the "young brothers" know how he would use my songs to impress the young ladies he had an interest in, showing them how "smooth" he was. After much laughter from the audience, the senator began to sing. Yes, he sang! "If you see me walking down the street" (in tune, I might add), giving a bit of advice after each verse—"and I start to cry"—and showing he had rhythm by swaying as he sang—"Walk on by."

Well, to be serenaded by the man who is now the president of the United States of America was quite something and will long be remembered. And it's all on film. In fact, you can catch it on YouTube.

I truly believed Barack Obama would become America's first African American president. And I am so very proud that he is actively trying to fulfill the promise of change we are so desperately in need of here in this United States of America. I honestly believe that before his terms (yes, I pluralized "term") are up, he will have done exactly what he promised to do. He exemplifies the values that have somehow become lost here, the values of family, respect of elders, and bringing out the best we Americans have to offer. President Obama is dedicated to restoring America to its position as a respected world leader, a nation of people who, by working together, can fulfill all the promise our great country offers.

He believes that he can wake us up enough to get this done, and so do I.

I truly admire all of these extraordinary people, and I am very humbled to have had them touch my life. They are my sources of inspiration.

CHAPTER 12

Superwomen: Dream Team

WORKING WITH friends, as mentioned earlier, is something that I truly enjoy, and lead me to the work with my "sisters" Gladys Knight and Patti LaBelle on a recording titled "Superwoman" in 1991.

Gladys called both of us to be a part of her recording and video shoot of this song. We went into the studio, recorded, and had a ball doing it. Doing a video shoot was new to me, and at this point it was something I felt belonged to the youngsters who were now dominating the industry. In my mind, videos were their tool for promoting their recordings, something not really for my generation. But we had the best time doing the video. We laughed all the way through and wondered if and where it would ever be played beyond our own VCRs.

The song and video turned out great. Gladys was invited to appear on the *Oprah* show and asked if Patti and I would come on as well to perform "Superwoman." We did and the reception from the audience was incredible. Oprah asked all of the appropriate questions regarding the song and the recording process.

Oprah referred to us as the "Dream Team." And if doing quality work in the recording studio for many decades is the measure and not money—then we were. When folks see us appearing on television shows, they may think that we are earning millions of dollars when in fact we're paid something called "scale" for our appearances, which can amount to the incredible sum of approximately $300, depending on the type of show we are on. Neither our record company nor the entertainment industry at large treated us like a dream team. Our wonderful record and video weren't given a chance to be competitive. I sometimes think we should have said that on *Oprah,* but we took the high road. With our then collective 155 years of experience in the business, our legacy and contributions will prevail in the long run.

One very valuable lesson I've learned through the years is that no matter what your career is or isn't, it's very important to think and plan long term. The truth is that success—no matter how grand— will dissipate over time.

Those who are now dominating in the industry are fortunate to have the added promotional tool of the visual to help sell their recordings. For their sakes, I hope that they are smart enough to know that they are always as good as their current hit and must keep this stream going or they, like me, will be dependent upon their ability to travel and perform live.

DIONNE'S LESSONS LEARNED

- *Success will dissipate over time.*

CHAPTER 13

Déjà Vu

A FTER BEING on one of the most incredible highs of my career during the mid- to late '80s, I learned the true meaning of the "peaks and valleys" in the career of an artist again in the 1990s.

Music and the public's taste for certain music was changing. Hip-hop was taking over the airwaves, and something that was being called "the new R&B" was also pushing those of us who had created what I guess you would call "the old R&B" and pop completely off the playlists. In addition, the playlist had dwindled so that fewer records were being heard. Many of the independent radio stations across the country were now being acquired by major corporations, so what artist and which songs were played on the air became a centralized corporation decision.

You heard none of the beautiful sounds of Johnny Mathis, Barbra Streisand, or the soulful sounds of Gladys Knight, Patti LaBelle, Smokey Robinson, the Temptations, Earth, Wind and Fire, and the O'Jays—even though these artists all continued to make music that was as good as, sometimes even better than, what they were best known for. These were among the many artists who had paved the way for all of those enjoying success with radio airplay, but had now been abandoned by radio, and that list included me. Fortunately, for those of us who came up in the industry with the ability to sing and perform live, we could still draw an audience for our shows.

It was during this time that my recording contract with Arista was coming to an end. As with all of the other recording companies, Arista had become more oriented toward a younger market, adding to its roster the likes of the wonderful Alicia Keys and my cousin Whitney Houston, to name a few. Arista was fast leading the way once again within the record industry. Unfortunately, as the record industry changed, the old tradition of continuing to record and promote respected "legacy" artists was abandoned, and the entire focus shifted to finding a smaller number of "bigger" young artists. Instead of looking to a roster of twenty artists who could each have a couple of hits from an album, the record companies wanted just a handful of artists who could produce three, four, five, even six hits from a single album. This "blockbuster" mentality left no room for artists like me or many of my talented peers.

Even though the reasons for this second "lull" in my career were different from the first, for me it was déjà vu all over again.

I had a record in the marketplace but not a hit. And my concert fee began to dip a bit as a result. So when I was asked by a friend, Marge Cowan, to host a television pilot being shot with a psychic named Linda Georgian, I considered it. Marge, now deceased, told me the hosting role would be just for the pilot and would pay me very well. The pilot was called *The Psychic Friends Network*. It was a fun time for me, and I thought it might be a fun project to work on as I was always attracted to astrology, numerology, fortune-tellers, and psychics. I've always believed there were special people who had gifts and were able to foresee the future.

Because I had the experience of being a hostess of the show *Solid Gold,* being the hostess of this would be a piece of cake. Or so I thought.

I did the pilot and it was being shown as an infomercial very late at night and we—the producers, Linda, and I—never believed it would take off like it did. It became the number one infomercial of its kind, and that meant we had a show that could—and did—run for quite a while. I guess once again I pioneered the way. But being first at anything does not always lead to being heaped with praise. I was paid very well, but I wish I had negotiated a much better contract with a clause giving me a bit of ownership. At the time, however, who knew the success the show would have? Then all of a sudden, people began thinking that I was a psychic. I was amused until I found myself having to explain publicly that I was merely the host of the show and was not positioning myself as a psychic. Some people acted as if I had done something sacrilegious when in fact all I was doing was making an honest living with a very, very good payday.

Linda was the psychic on the show. My job was merely to open the show by welcoming the viewers and introducing her. Those who had the notion that I was the psychic apparently had not watched the show closely. Anyone who watched for five minutes knew that Linda was the one doing the psychic stuff and I was the one with the microphone in the audience taking the questions being asked of her.

Members of my church looked at me as if I had the plague. The "mothers" of the church were the worst ones, saying things like "How can you do this? You are a Christian and should know better."

These were the kind of hypocrites you find in every church—and I had finally had my fill. I confess that I was a bit disrespectful to one of those "holier than thou" ladies when I reminded her that she told me of a young man who had been born with a "veil" over his face. Now, this was supposed to mean that he had a gift of being able to "foresee the future," according to her (duh). After I gave her back the words she had said to me, she immediately became one of my biggest allies, and when anyone else said anything about me with regard to the show, she was the first to come to my defense.

Many times walking through airports, shopping in the supermarket, or just walking down the street, I would be stopped and asked to tell the one who stopped me their "future." Of course, after this happened so frequently, I decided to start having fun and began saying things like "I see you will wake up in the morning and your hair will be standing up all over your head."

There was also an incident where a very elderly lady stopped me and went on and on about how I shouldn't be doing this. I asked if she knew her astrological sign, and she told me what it was. I said, "Aha." I then asked if she watched the show, and she said she did. And I couldn't resist; I got serious and asked her what she was doing up that late at night. She didn't have an answer. I think I caught her off guard.

Let's set the record straight. No, I am not a psychic and I have never been one. If I were, I would be sitting atop a mountain with a huge ruby on my forehead, without a care in the world.

I finally stopped defending my reason for doing the show and with each criticism would pose the question: Are you going to pay my bills? It took quite some time after the *Psychic Friends Network* show went off the air before certain attitudes about what people thought I was doing began to subside.

My primary objective was to take care of my family. I was earning an honest living by hosting the show, which I don't regret doing. It was obvious that nobody was going to pay my mortgage, provide food for my household, clothe my children, pay my housekeeper, my staff, and all the rest of my bills—many of the same ones you have: lights, gas, water, you know the drill—all of the essentials of survival. Moreover, my concern was to provide long-term financial security for my family.

I'm a celebrity, yes. But I put my jeans on like you do—one leg at a time.

CHAPTER 14

The End of an Era

THE GREAT record producer Arif Mardin and I had a wonderful experience working on a "Cole Porter Project." Arif, the legendary producer and twelve-time Grammy Award winner, had the brilliant idea of making a jazz-inflected album, and we did the first version in this fashion. We both loved it and handed it in to Clive Davis, the head of Arista. Well, this was not what Clive had in mind. We were told it sounded too much like a cabaret recording and that Clive wanted more of a ballroom kind of sound with lush strings, so off we went to rerecord. We came back with something more to Clive's liking. The sound was beautiful but, in both Arif's and my opinion, very vanilla. But the head honcho was happy, and the project was released.

Clive was, once again, right. He has an absolute ear of uncanny proportions and a track record for knowing the marketplace and the record-buying public's choices. I received the first Cole Porter

"You're the Top" Award and still get requests to sing songs from this project.

I anxiously played it for Ella Fitzgerald and looked for signs of either approval or disapproval in her face. When she finished listening, she took both of my hands in hers and smiled, saying she did really like it. Nothing could have pleased me more.

I toured with the London Philharmonic Orchestra throughout the United Kingdom doing an evening of Cole Porter music, and it was very well received. What followed were three other studio projects. I flew to England to record and be produced by Lisa Stansfield, who had asked if she could produce me. Lisa is a white British singer who topped pop and R&B charts everywhere in the early '90s with hits such as "All Around the World." Clive agreed that it was a good idea, but I hated this project. I did not feel the songs or production met the standard that I was accustomed to. The one song that I still feel uncomfortable even mentioning is titled "Where My Lips Have Been." It was a lot—not a little—outside of the messages I was known to deliver lyrically, and I think it tested me to the brink.

The album was titled *Friends Can Be Lovers,* and I felt this song and the majority of the songs on it were songs Lisa should have recorded herself. The album did not sell well at all, and I believe if she had recorded these songs they would have fared much better.

On the other hand, I loved recording *Aquarela do Brasil* (in Portuguese, Brazil is spelled with an *s*). This project took me to Brazil to work with Teo Lima. He served as producer and gave me some of the greatest musicians to work with and songs that were recognized not only in Brazil but also worldwide. I knew that not everybody would be familiar with the titles of the songs, but once they heard the music, they would recognize them. Even when I show off and sing in Portuguese, the audiences seem to act as if they understand every word.

The songwriters were Antonio Carlos Jobim, Dori Caymmi, Chico Buarque and Edu Lobo, Brenda Russell, and the late Ary Barroso. I even asked Burt and Hal to write a song, and after years of not speaking to each other, they came through for me. Eliana Estevao, who was at the time one of my background singers, coached me with Portuguese pronunciation, and I even translated into English a few of the songs, one being the very sensuous "Oh Bahia."

Once the rhythm tracks and vocals were finished, Teo came to Los Angeles where the strings, horns, and backgrounds were recorded. I was working with Dori Caymmi, Oscar Castro-Neves, and John Williams, who were all writing beautiful string and horn arrangements. Brenda Russell arranged and provided some of the greatest background vocalists in Los Angeles. I knew I had a winner.

So I was surprised to learn that Clive and the Arista promotion team were not enthused. I was puzzled when it became apparent that they weren't promoting the record the way I thought it should be, because it certainly fit the label and lent itself to the kind of promotion of, let's say, a Kenny G project. I guess I should have been a bit stronger with my suggestions for how to promote it.

My relationship with the label was beginning to feel like my previous one with Warner Bros. Once again, I was caught in the midst of internal change and was fast becoming the "step-child." So I left Arista shortly after *Aquarela do Brasil* was released in 1994.

Rhino Records, a division of Warner Bros., acquired many of my Scepter, Warner, and Arista recordings, giving their special products division license to release a ton of compilation CDs on me. It got to the point that the market was so flooded with these compilations that I finally asked if they would put a curb on it. I believe they understood, because they did begin to lessen those releases.

Once again, without a record company or product, I relied on my status as an entertainer. The beauty of my Arista tryst is that Clive and I remain very close friends and still have a great deal of respect and care for each other.

CHAPTER 15

What the World Needs Now

IN THE late '70s and early '80s, the Sugarhill Gang, Kurtis Blow, Grandmaster Flash and the Furious Five, Run-D.M.C., L.L. Cool J, Kool Moe Dee, and a few other artists were responsible for rap and hip-hop finding a place in the industry. They took the African American musical traditions of call and response, scatting, "the dozens," and syncopated, jazzed-up rhymes done by icons like Cab Calloway, who would use rhythm and rhyme playfully in their music, to a whole new level. That was fine, but in the coming years, as hip-hop became a true force in the business, the genre evolved into something known as "gangsta rap." Groups and individuals sprung up like wildfire—Bone Thugs-N-Harmony, Kurupt, N.W.A, Snoop Dogg, Dr. Dre, Ice-T, Ice Cube, Tupac Shakur, Biggie Smalls, and too many more—and started using curse words that the Federal Communications Commission would never have allowed to be played on radio in the past. For some reason, suddenly the FCC was now turning a deaf ear. I was angered as I heard children on street

corners singing these offensive lyrics that glorified pimps, drug deal-
ers, gang members, murderers, and violence. Many young girls and
grown women were also enjoying music that called them bitches
and whores, and actually laughing aloud, as if this were funny or
"cool." How could we have allowed this to happen?

I remember riding in my car with my youngest son, Damon,
when one of those recordings (I, like the late Ray Charles, refuse
to refer to them as "songs") came on the radio and he began to
sing along. When I pulled the car over and asked how he knew the
words, he said that he had been hearing that recording and many
more like it on the radio. I let him know that those words were not
in the vocabulary that I wanted him to use, as they were demeaning
and insulting, especially to girls his age and ladies like his mommy.
I asked if he thought of me in the terms that were being used in the
records.

This was not the kind of language he had heard in our home,
and I did not want him to think that at age sixteen (or any other
age) it was all right to say those kinds of things. He understood and
promised he would heed what I said. The message was an important
one for him to hear, since he was interested in becoming a record
producer. By the time he was eighteen he was offered the opportunity to record the group Bone Thugs-N-Harmony, one of those at
the forefront of gangsta rap. I didn't know it at the time and would
not have discovered this new development except that I decided to
visit the recording studio one night.

I walked in as Flesh-n-Bone, a featured performer of the group,
was putting his voice on a track. I stood in the doorway of the room
in total shock. When Damon realized that I was standing there, I
thought my child was going to have a heart attack. He immediately
called a break and took me outside of the studio. I was hurt that he

broke his promise. Before he could explain, I said to him that we would discuss the matter when he came home. And we did.

He had been asked to create tracks (beats) for the group to record over and had been paid to engineer the recording as well. He also told me that he had created tracks for Kurupt and a few other rappers. But, he said, he would not continue to work with them.

I know I may have ruined his ability to make a lot of money, but I couldn't consent to this. I was not only opposed to the messages of gangsta rap and my son being involved, but I was also working with C. Delores Tucker, a notable civil rights activist and the head of the National Political Congress of Black Women (now the National Congress of Black Women). She had issued a call to free the airwaves of these degrading and negative words that influence all, but especially children who looked up to these artists.

During one of the meetings of the National Political Congress of Black Women, an open invitation went out to enlist other African American women within the recording industry to become involved in this struggle. Melba Moore and Anita Baker signed on immediately. I must say that I was disappointed that more of my peers seemed afraid to become involved, but this was understandable, I guess.

C. Delores and the National Political Congress of Black Women organized a full-out campaign with interviews and press conferences. C. Delores accomplished a coup when she bought stock in Time Warner. This allowed her to participate in discussions of the matter as a stockholder of the parent company that was in business with Suge Knight, president of Death Row Records. In 1995, while at a National Political Congress of Black Women conference in Seattle, I was told that Suge Knight had been invited to meet with C. Delores and me to discuss how changes could be made to the content of these recordings without destroying the core of their messages.

He agreed to meet with me in my home in Beverly Hills, along with a few of his recording artists. Both of my sons thought I had really lost it when I told them. But knowing their mother, they knew I was serious. I set this meeting for seven in the morning, and Suge and the others were all at my front door not a minute late.

I must say I was surprised. Not that they showed up, but that they showed up at that hour of the morning and on time. I had coffee and Danish ready for them, and we sat in my living room and began our talk. I started by letting them know what I considered to be a problem and asked how I could be part of the solution.

They told me that they thought C. Delores and I were "dissing" them. Of course, I had no idea what that term meant and asked them to explain. Suge said it meant "disrespecting." I simply asked why they could not have said this in the beginning, and I am still waiting for an answer.

Be that as it may, we continued our meeting and we discussed how I felt that they were all being exploited and being used by Interscope Records, the subsidiary of the parent company of Time Warner and the parent company of Death Row. I also said that the amount of money Suge made from this music may have seemed like a lot, but he should compare it to the amount of money being made by Time Warner. We called Time Warner to pose this question to their representatives, and as it would happen, they were in a meeting with their board and stockholders. And guess who was there? C. Delores Tucker, a Time Warner stockholder, making her point regarding this very issue.

She came armed with album covers, "lyrics"—I use this word cautiously—and photographs, stating that these were the kinds of things being promoted throughout *our* neighborhoods and not those neighborhoods of whites. She reminded her colleagues at Time Warner that she was a product of the civil rights movement and knew how to put loudspeakers and bullhorns on trucks to demonstrate against the rise of gangsta rap in the same communities record companies targeted with their marketing.

Suge said in our meeting that he thought there could be something done to address the problem and that he would give it some thought. I again made it clear that I wasn't against their intended message in the music, but that I objected to the language. After I ordered lunch for us, it seemed as if I had made them understand where I was coming from and that I was not in fact "dissing" them.

I testified before Congress on this issue. The chair was Senator Carol Moseley Braun, and members of Congress were present along with some of the rap community: Snoop Dogg, N.W.A, Dr. Dre, and record executives who produced and distributed these recordings. When asked to speak, I was brief and to the point, letting all know my disappointment in the record companies' exploitation of these kids, and how I felt the airwaves were polluting my ears and the ears of children with this kind of exposure to the words and actions heard on these recordings.

Representative Maxine Waters (someone I referred to as one of my girlfriends) considered this a First Amendment issue and defended the artists' right to express themselves. My mouth dropped open. I challenged her by reminding her that as a female with a daughter and a granddaughter, she might consider my position on the issue. I was certain she personally would not want to be referred to as a bitch or whore, and certainly would not want her daughter or granddaughter to be thought of in this way either. There was no further response from her. I believe this may have been one of those times when both sides of the aisle were able to agree on something.

One of the characteristics of this particular music culture was competition. While I always felt competition was healthy, however, I thought the "East Coast rappers vs. West Coast rappers" thing was senseless. Two truly brilliant young men, Tupac Shakur and Biggie Smalls, were probably murdered as a consequence of this competition. In an effort to unite the hip-hop community in 1998, I recorded with the Hip Hop Nation United a version of "What the World Needs Now." My objective was to demonstrate cooperation with the community of rappers using the medium that we all loved. I was with a record company called River North at this time, and they were all for my trying to make this happen (I know they never believed it would happen). My son Damon was not convinced it could happen either, but he helped along with Angelo Ellerbee, the chief executive officer of the public relations firm I was with at the time, Double XXposure.

To everyone's surprise, Big Daddy Kane, Bobby Brown, Horace Brown, Mike City, Coolio, Flesh-n-Bone, Mic Geronimo, Tony Grant, Ray J, Mechalie Jamison, Kurupt, Royal Flush, Tyrese, and Veronica all signed on to this project, and what a wonderful recording it is. They all adhered to the rule forbidding any profanity. I asked that they each write down their response to the meaning of the song as they saw it. I am as proud of this recording as I am of any of the others I've made.

Damon created and produced the track and made me so proud. I earned the respect of all the participating artists, whom I still refer to as "my babies." They gave me the name of "Auntie D" and "Mommy D." We also appeared together on the nationwide television show *The View*.

Hip-hop has grown up since those days, like the Virginia Slims cigarettes slogan that says, "You've come a long way, baby." I'm proud of how the genre has developed, including more positive content, language, and presentation.

The music may not be my cup of tea, but the artists have grown up to become ladies and gentlemen who are paving the way for our children and, in many cases, our grown-ups, all by example. It's ironic that this has happened in a relatively short period, and all "for the greater good."

Dana Owens, better known as Queen Latifah, has grown from the rough and tough rapper to being nominated for an Academy Award as an actress; she has a star on the Hollywood Walk of Fame and is a successful entrepreneur. Dana has always had positive things to say, and she has bloomed into a world-class beauty. She, too, has taken her fame and used it as a torch burning bright, serving as a model of progress and accomplishment for her fans. I am exceptionally proud of this young lady, as she proudly hails from my hometown of East Orange. She has gone from being known as a rapper to also being known as a singing recording artist (and, I will add, she is a very good singer). Dana's ride to success has been steadily paced. She has carefully climbed up the ladder of success.

I met the members of Destiny's Child when they were still in their teen years through my son Damon, who produced some of their early recordings. All of the girls are very talented in their own way and give us music that is catchy with lyrics that are appropriate for all ages. But Beyoncé has gone on to reach heights that I don't believe even she imagined were possible. A triple threat, she not only has honed her craft in the area of singing, recording, and writing but now produces her own recordings as well. She and her mother, Tina Knowles, founded House of Deréon, named after Beyoncé's grandmother, a talented seamstress. Together they have built a successful couture clothing line. Brilliantly managed by her father, Mathew Knowles, Beyoncé has also become a film star. What I find most pleasant is that she has remained grounded and has not allowed her success to "go to her head."

Again, Mary J. Blige has truly come a long way, too: from combat boots to Jimmy Choo shoes; from army and navy clothing to Armani; from rhinestones to Harry Winston jewels. Without a doubt, she wears it well. Her recording career is amazing and still on the rise. Her songwriting is full of growth-giving messages of hope, love, and faith.

Many of the men in hip-hop today have become moguls, owning sports teams, restaurants, fashion lines, fragrances, sneakers, drinks of all kinds inclusive of liquors, and the list goes on.

Puffy, Puff Daddy, Diddy, or as I know him, Sean Combs, came from a rap background, selling his records out of the trunks of cars. Then he had the good fortune to meet Andre Harrell, a mentor who gave him the courage to believe he could do anything that he wanted to in this business. He also has a mother who encouraged, nurtured, and kept him believing in himself. He has built an empire to rival any other and has done it by using his brain. He has conquered the record industry, the film industry, the Broadway stage, the fashion world, the fragrance world, and I believe if he put his mind to it and had a desire to do so he could also find a new way to exploit outer space.

Jay-Z., Shawn Carter (I think the name Shawn, no matter how it's spelled, must be lucky), is another inspiring figure from the rap community who has become a huge success, using his accomplishments to offer opportunities that benefit others. He also has ownership in areas that were thought to be out of his reach, such as the New Jersey Nets basketball team and his $150 million deal with Live Nation, the premier concert promotion company. He recently tied the knot with Beyoncé and I'd say he is a very happy young man and does his part to spread the happiness.

And the one who surprised everybody, including me, is 50 Cent, Curtis Jackson, the mogul. His recordings still sell in massive amounts; his business sense has taken him to a $400 million payout when Coca-Cola purchased the company that makes Vitaminwater. He too is in the clothing business (G-Unit), has a record label, is a film star, has sold millions of video games, and at this writing may have completed his deal with South African billionaire Patrice Motsepe as a partner in mining. He is definitely on a roll and has turned his life around.

I also love the fact that all of these young men have had mention in *Forbes* magazine noting their entrepreneurial and financial wherewithal.

These young men and women have become what is known as a successful "brand" (which could be a name, an image, or symbol). They also each possess something that's very important: a positive "attitude" in believing "I can, I will, and I did."

I'd like to think that their rise to success was somewhat derived from me and my peers—Tina Turner, Gladys Knight, Patti LaBelle, Diana Ross, Aretha Franklin, just to name a few. We have all given them our shoulders to stand on as they were coming up in this business. But, unlike them, we did not take total advantage of ourselves as "brands." No one was really using that term when our careers were on the rise. The idea of marketing oneself beyond the records and the concerts was not widely practiced for most African American artists (or, when it was, African American artists rarely benefited as they should have) However, during this period, there were some white artists who successfully exploited and benefited from this (branding) concept.

These doors of opportunity, which we didn't realize were there for us, I'm thrilled to say, have been kicked wide open by this generation. And I'm very proud of them.

Everyone should think of themselves as a "brand." You don't have to be in show business for that. It's about knowing yourself and having an attitude and a belief in yourself and your ability to succeed. Consider every aspect of your personality and values: the way you dress, the way you speak, and the way you walk or, as I like to term it, "swagger." This is simply how holding your head high gives the feel and look of confidence not only to others but (look in the mirror) to yourself, too. Since I have been described as being elegant, classy, with the signature voice, this has become my brand along with my name and likeness.

The object is to market yourself as a brand versus marketing yourself as a product. Those I have described are brands; they don't simply sell records or concert tickets—they sell themselves as a "brand."

My business partner, coauthor, and dear friend David Freeman Wooley is also an adjunct professor of business and marketing at Wilmington University. He's been keeping me up to date in these areas of business. Dave taught me about IMC (Integrated Marketing Communication), which, in short, is unifying your marketing efforts.

In retrospect, I think that President Obama utilized this marketing process while he was campaigning. He was consistent with his message of "Change" and he integrated the phrase "Yes We Can" in some of his speeches and ads. This is what these young folks all have been—consistent. They consistently deliver by looking the part, walking the walk, and talking the talk, and by producing a cohesive, consistent message. It's synergy.

I've learned that whatever I'm doing in business or marketing, I should strive to be better than my competitor. Also, while utilizing the media outlets of radio, television, print, or the Internet (viral marketing), I'm mindful that time is money. Moreover, I make sure that my time is managed when I'm giving interviews, doing promotional tours, or press junkets, and the like.

In sum, Dave also taught me how to do a SWOT analysis. It's an acronym for Strengths, Weaknesses, Opportunities, and Threats. Honestly, I'd never analyzed my work this way before. However, if you are working on a plan (or project), it's a good business tool that can help you analyze, identify, address, and evaluate what you're working on. For example (briefly stated), make a list of the internal Strengths of your plan, the internal Weaknesses, external Opportunities, and the external Threats.

You see—it's never too late to be a student.

DIONNE'S LESSONS LEARNED

- *Think of yourself as a brand.*

- *Dress, speak, and walk with swagger.*

- *Believe that you can and you are.*

- *Be humble and be consistent.*

CHAPTER 16

A Mother's Love

HAVE TWO wonderful and exceptional sons. And I know all those reading this who have children of their own feel exactly this way about their children, too.

David, my eldest, was born January 18, 1969, and, like me, he decided to make his entrance into the world two months early. My mother told me the way the first child is born usually follows the pattern of how the mother was born; I was a seven-month baby, too. Mommy also told me I was just nosy and that is the reason I appeared before time.

Anyway, when I started having labor pains, I called my doctor, who was out of town. The doctor covering for him told me that I couldn't be having labor pains because I was just seven months along, and that he thought it had to be gas. He wanted me to take an Alka-Seltzer to calm my stomach down. I did what he told me to do and it subsided a bit, but only for a few minutes.

The pain started again. Daddy was still working as a Pullman porter and was out of town. And Bill was in Pittsburgh working at a club. Nobody expected me to go into labor two months ahead of time. My uncle Sonny happened to be at our house, so he and my mother got me bundled up to get to the hospital. I pulled my beautiful mink coat over my flannel pajamas—of all things. But, being in show business, I had to put on my lashes and a bit of foundation. As I was in the bathroom making my face, a *major* pain hit me and I made a beeline for the door, got in my uncle's car, and we were off to the Presbyterian Hospital in Newark.

On the way, my uncle found every pothole in the street, and I thought I was going to have my baby in his car. We arrived at the hospital, Mommy answered all of the necessary questions, and I was taken straightaway to the maternity ward. I expected to see my doctor, but he was in Bimini, fishing. The hospital did reach him, though, and he gave them instructions on what to do until he got back.

David had breached and decided he would stay in my tummy for a little while longer. In so doing, he had wrapped the umbilical cord around his neck. This was why the pain was so bad and why I could not be given anything to relieve it. Bill rushed back and got there before David was born.

And fortunately, Dr. Burch had his own plane and got back to Newark in time to tend to me and my baby. I was very groggy when Dr. Burch brought the baby to me, telling me to look at what I had done. All I remember saying is, "He looks like an old man." And he did.

David was not a pretty baby at all. It may sound strange to hear his mother say it, but that's the way it was. He and I stayed in the hospital for two weeks afterward. Since he was premature, they wanted to make sure that he was doing okay. And during that period, he began to fill out and he actually did become cute.

Once we were home, I would sit by his crib and watch him, making sure he was breathing. Taking care of him was not as easy as I thought it would be. My mother tried to help, but I became a bit testy. "I can take care of my baby," I said to her. She in turn smiled and said, "Okay, but let me give you just a little piece of advice, young lady." She said, "David is not a doll and when he is sleeping, you should sleep. Otherwise, you'll be spending a lot of time awake." I not only learned that her advice had merit, but soon realized it might not be such a bad idea to have Mommy come stay with me for a while. She did, and I finally got a complete night's sleep.

My pregnancy with Damon was different. He decided before he left my body that he did not want me to work. I had evening sickness instead of morning sickness and that did not go very well with having to perform at night. I remember being at Harrah's in Lake Tahoe and as my music to enter started, I walked onstage only to have to make a very hasty exit. Once I got myself together, I explained to the audience that the child I was carrying apparently did not have a desire to be in show business. This was a constant—and I finally had to come off the road until he was born. Ironically, it is Damon who is now one of the most sought-after record producers in the industry and who travels extensively with recording artists all over the world. Go figure.

By the time Damon was born on March 21, 1973, I pretty much had a handle on being Mommy. It was becoming a bit easier. But things weren't so easy when Damon was nine months old, because Bill and I were then divorcing. I had to get back on the road to keep the lights on, you know. I didn't have my mother to help me at first. She was in New Jersey with no desire to come to Los Angeles. But she did get over her fear of earthquakes and came out and stayed until I hired someone to help. That person was Julia Boutte, a petite little thing whom I consider an angel that the good Lord dropped into my life. David was in the kitchen during my interview of Julia. I was preparing to go grocery shopping and she volunteered to go for me. (She drove, too? Yes, luck was with me.) David asked me if he could go with her. Well, I couldn't believe my ears; my son did not typically warm up to people right away. So that was how I knew she was the right person to care for my children. Her credentials were stellar. She had cared for the children of Lou Costello and Bob Hope, and had taken care of Steve Allen's home for years.

Julia was able to start immediately and became a part of the family. I felt quite comfortable being able to leave my babies with her while I went back on the road. She made sure my boys were involved with everything I wanted them to be. I wanted them to learn sports, baseball, football, hockey, and I wanted them to be able to ride horses, fish, play tennis, ride bikes. It was a joy to go to the sporting games they played and watch their growth as they became teens. Fortunately, the majority of my friends happen to be male and they were of tremendous help, too.

We lived for a while in Aspen, Colorado, where they both learned to ski and became a part of ski patrol. That's how good they both are. Damon became a very good hockey player, and David became good enough at skiing to be looked at for Olympic consideration as a downhill racer. Andy Mill, a gold-medal-winning Olympic downhill racer, wanted to train David, but I thought it was too dangerous and felt skiing for pleasure would be enough. During this time, we enjoyed having a big Saint Bernard, who we affectionately named Tiny. We moved back to Los Angeles after living in Aspen for five years. The boys were both enrolled in Fishburne Military School in Waynesboro, Virginia, along with my nephew Barry.

But Fishburne was not David's cup of tea, and he asked if he could go to another type of school. It was a reasonable request, so we went school hunting and found a school that he was happy with: Cushing Academy, just outside of the Boston area. And it was coed (aha). Damon and Barry both graduated from Fishburne, and David graduated from Cushing. They all attended college and have grown into the most incredible family men.

I have six grandchildren. David's wife had two children (Mandela and Maya) from a previous relationship. David fathered two daughters. Cheyenne, who at this writing is fifteen, is gorgeous and has a voice to be reckoned with. She has appeared with me on my tours during the summer months, and if she so desires she can be an important entertainer. She has a wonderful personality. She also has great stage presence and—just as I could when I was an emerging singer—she can "close a show." Lealand is four years old at this writing and is my little "Camille." I think she will be the actress.

Damon's wife had one child (Neko) prior to their relationship. Damon fathered one daughter, Kaelyn, who is now eleven. I believe she will be my fashion model. She loves those things that "girly" girls gravitate to: long hair, designer clothing and accessories—they learn early—and lip gloss. And they are all gorgeous. Once again, I received the gift of the girls I never had through my sons. Both sons compose and have great voices. Damon's interest remains the same in that he is still producing recordings for artists of today and is working on developing a television show of inspirational value. David is now traveling on the road with me opening my shows. During their early growing years, my personal appearances schedule was set around their school projects. I was a part of the bake sales at Hawthorne, their elementary school. I attended every school play and I even carpooled. Now the kids loved it when I was able to do this.

In fact, I earned the nickname "Marion Andretti" and loved "zoom-ing" them to school. My house became "Hotel 806" because of the many sleeping bags that I would have to step over when I would come home after a tour. There were times when I had to become the disciplinarian, as Julia could be a bit soft. I remember having to come home from Las Vegas one afternoon because of a water bal-loon incident that David had gotten himself involved in.

Somehow, in his youthful mind, David thought it would be fun to throw water balloons out the window onto moving cars. I guess he said to himself, "Mommy is in Las Vegas working—so I think I'll just lose my mind." When I got the phone call, I immediately chartered a private plane to Los Angeles, then took a limousine to my house, where I took care of some "mommy business" with my son. Well, when he saw me walk through that door still wearing my sequined stage gown, his eyes almost jumped out of his face. He kept shaking, and I thought he had completely lost it. He was startled and bewildered, to say the least. I flew back to Vegas, just in time to walk onstage and take care of some "show business." My actions showed both David and Damon that I was only a phone call and plane ride away, and I would and could take care of *any* situa-tion without any problem.

Damon had his share of mischief, too. He and one of his friends thought it was cool that they could sneak into Disneyland unde-tected, or so they thought. So once again, I received a call and I flew in and quickly took care of the situation. Both of my sons knew that when punishments had to be handed out, I firmly stood by them to the fullest extent. There was never a problem as my children came of age with drinking or drugs, and I'm most grateful for that. David even became a police officer. He served with the Whittier, Cali-fornia, Police Department for a while and also with the Hermosa

Beach Police Department. I wasn't so thrilled about him choosing this line of work. I was of course nervous. But he was happy and was an excellent officer, though I admit that I am relieved that he decided to get back to music. The appearance of gray strands in my hair slowed down as well. I have also passed the "torch" on to both of my sons.

Over the years, I have learned that our children are mirror images of us, and whatever they hear and see within their home environment will become a vital part of what they will eventually say and do. Both of my guys were introduced to church early in their lives and the importance of having God as their guide was important. They both know the words and worth of prayer, and I am so very proud that they raise their own children to lead spiritual lives.

"I love my children."
(Personal collection of Dionne Warwick)

We speak practically every day. And ever since they were little bitty people, our conversation—in person or on the phone—always ends with "I love you."

DIONNE'S LESSONS LEARNED

- *Our children are mirror images of ourselves.*

- *It's important to have God in the lives of children.*

CHAPTER 17

Awards/Rewards and the Legends Ball

B EING REWARDED brings a lot of joy, especially when it is for the things that come naturally. I've humbly received many awards and rewards for my life and work, such as the People's Choice Award, five Grammys, gold and platinum albums, the East Orange General Hospital Achievement Award, and many more. I had the honor of being appointed the Ambassador of Health for the United States and the Goodwill Ambassador of the Food and Agriculture Organization (FAO) section of the United Nations.

I received my star on the Walk of Fame in Hollywood on my birthday, December 12, 1985. The then mayor of Los Angeles, Tom Bradley, extended the formal congratulations in such loving and glowing words that I thought I'd burst with pride. And the presence of my mother, sister, two sons, and a gang of my friends put the cherry on top of that wonderful cake. I've been asked about the top

I wore that day. It was silver and black (Oakland Raiders colors) and had the number 12 on it, signifying my birth date.

I visit my star and also take a cloth to keep it clean. If you want to visit my star, it is located between two major icons, Aretha Franklin and the Lone Ranger. And I have jokingly said, "Now all who thought they could walk over me can now do it, and I won't mind."

The National Association of Record Merchandisers Chairman's Award for Sustained Creative Achievement was presented to me in 1998. This meant the record merchandisers thought the recordings I had done were of ultimate quality, and that is quite something given the number of records released during the course of a year. To know that mine were actually the very best is an awesome reward.

The History Makers Award is one that I will always cherish as it is given to African Americans acknowledged to have made a difference in the world for the better. To be put in the company of those who have been given this honor, and for it to be given to me by my own, an African American organization, can never be beat. This is something we as African Americans all look for, and that is approval from our own communities. And when that recognition is given, it's a feeling that can never be described in just a few words.

The Red Ribbon Foundation Award: what can I say? I've been working on the AIDS issue for more than thirty years and I'm still very much involved with agencies worldwide that are tirelessly giving time, expertise, money, and care to find a way to stem this disease until an absolute cure is found.

I applaud all of those organizations and agencies, and they know without a doubt they can "always count on me." I will say proudly that I wish I had enough wall space and shelf space in my home to house all the rewards I have received.

To be thought of by the industry and to be rewarded with an

honor such as the Heroes Award, given by the New York chapter of the Recording Academy, is quite humbling.

Our industry does not just decide to honor anyone without doing full, in-depth research of the history of the person they are considering honoring. And to think that I may have done things that would want the industry to consider me for the award makes me know that the work I do and the body of work that speaks for me is merit enough to receive such an honor as this. I guess, like Dorothy in *The Wizard of Oz,* I was able to click my heels three times and successfully make it home. Mommy, my son David, Clive Davis, Burt, and Hal were all there to applaud my honor with me that night in 2002. And the wonderful part about walking to the stage to receive it was that it was being presented to me by one of my best buddies, Luther Vandross, who had the biggest smile on his face when he handed it to me. Mommy and David both were bursting with pride, as were Clive, Burt, and Hal. It was truly a memorable evening.

I received the Rhythm & Blues Foundation's Pioneer Award for lifetime achievement in 2003 during a very posh evening affair in New York. Jerry Butler (remember, he's the one who recorded "Make It Easy on Yourself") presented it to me, and we had a laugh onstage when I mentioned the song and how angry I was at him and Bacharach and David for giving him my song. To be honored by a sector of the industry that never thought of me as an R&B singer was truly a surprise and much appreciated. I never thought that I would be recognized by my peers in this genre, as I was always thought of as a pop recording artist and somewhat "outside the box" in relation to other R&B recording artists. Being accepted by all whom I have always considered my peers, regardless of the boxes the industry and the media try to put us in, is always exciting and, yep, I was excited and grateful to receive this reward.

Another way of being rewarded and recognized in the African

American community is to have been fortunate enough to grace the cover of either *Ebony* magazine or *Jet* magazine. This accomplishment will put a little hop in your step because this meant that as an artist you had arrived. Johnson Publications is the home of these two prestigious magazines, and Mr. John H. Johnson and his wife, Eunice, epitomized class, pride, awareness, and style about and within the African American community. Although I have never been on the cover of *Ebony*, I have been featured several times on the cover of *Jet*, and have had many articles and interviews featured in *Jet*. Mrs. Johnson, a lady of style, grace, and class brought to our communities the Ebony Fashion Fair, featuring couture fashion houses from designers known worldwide, giving African American ladies what they could and should want to wear. Mr. Johnson dedicated his expertise to bringing the news important to the African American community that the mainstream media too often overlooked. He featured editorials on Dr. Martin Luther King Jr., Rosa Parks, political figures of world stature, and those entertainers who were doing great things in and out of show business. It is the one magazine that I look forward to getting in my mail, and I hope the standard set by these two wonderful human beings will continue to expand and promote awareness of the important things the African American community continues to do. Sadly, both have made their transitions, but their legacy lives on.

In 2007, I was one of the Trumpet Awards honorees. Some of the other wonderful people on this elite list of honorees were Michael Jordan, Percy E. Sutton, Toni Braxton, Clint Eastwood, Donnie McClurkin, CeCe Winans, and Quincy Jones. This was a spectacular gala event held at the Bellagio Hotel in Las Vegas. The president and CEO of the Trumpet Awards, Ms. Xernona Clayton, and her team did a wonderful job. However, the highlight of the event for me was when Nancy Wilson and Gladys Knight presented the award to me. That was very exciting.

I have been truly blessed to be on the receiving end of countless citations of achievements and keys to many cities. I'm still wondering what they open and have asked if any of the banks in those particular cities had locks that the presented key would open; but alas, the answer was always no. But knowing those keys opened the hearts of the folks living in all of those cities is enough for me. Proclamations, community plaques—all have given me a sense that the things that were important to me were also important to so many others.

I also treasure having been presented with honorary doctoral degrees by my alma mater, the Hartt College of Music, as well as by Bethune-Cookman University, Shaw University, Columbia College of Chicago, Lincoln College, the University of Maryland Eastern Shore, and the American Bar Association. One honor that I do believe ranks up there was the renaming of my grammar school for me. This kind of bestowal is not loosely thrown around and is one that is a reward earned. When that doctoral hood is placed over your head and laid on your shoulders, believe me, the weight of the obligation that goes with it is a very heavy thing. And with pride I say I am handling the weight.

'VE RECEIVED many acknowledgments, awards, and rewards in my life, but nothing has outdone the show of appreciation by Oprah. Oprah Winfrey's Legends Ball was discussed all over the media and around the country in 2006 for good reason: it was spectacular.

I was shocked when I received a beautiful engraved invitation requesting my presence at a weekend event in honor of me and twenty-four other amazing women. The invitation included a specific request to wear a combination of black and white for the formal evening. This, of course, gave me an excuse to go shopping and put myself on a V8 juice, lettuce, and lemon juice regime so that the new dress would fit just right. The honorees arrived in Santa Barbara from our respective locations by car and by plane. I was driven via limousine. I arrived at the beautiful Bacara Resort and Spa to find myself preregistered and left on my own for the evening.

The actual festivities started the following day with a reception at Oprah's home for the twenty-five honorees, who were called "the legends" plus the "young'uns." The young'uns were younger African American women who came to pay homage to the legends for their great contributions and were making their way to becoming legends.

Oprah's home and grounds elicited the oohs and aahs that you might imagine. *Grand* is an understatement. Words are inadequate as well to describe what it was like to be in a room with some of the most powerful women on the planet. Being reminded that I happen to know most of these women personally was mind-boggling, and seeing them all in one room at one time was a moment I will always remember and cherish. I still feel privileged to have been there. Michelle Obama was one of the guests, and neither she nor we knew what was in store for her in the years to follow.

Once we had gathered and spent some time greeting each other, we were escorted to an area at the bottom of the stairway in the front of the home to board trolleys that took us to yet another spectacular area of the property—a close second to Central Park in New York City is how I'd describe it—to take a group photo. The photographer said, "Ladies, this is history in the making," and I totally agree; it was a very historical moment. We went from there to a luncheon crossing what Oprah described as that "Bridge to Now."

Now, I have attended many luncheons and dinners of great note, including those at the White House, but this one outshone those. I believe Angela Bassett captured it beautifully when she said, "We were treated like queens." And that is exactly the feeling we all had.

Service was impeccable, we each had individual waiters, the food was scrumptious, and we were serenaded by Grammy Award winner John Legend singing "Ordinary People."

The reading of the poem "We Speak Your Names" written by Pearl Cleage was the emotional high point of the afternoon. There were more mascara-marked faces in that tent from the tears shed than I have ever seen on all of these women, including mine. To think words were put in the form of tribute to us in this manner still is overwhelming and will always be remembered and treasured.

Topping it all were the gifts given to each of the legends and the young'uns, too. What are a "girl's best friend"? Yep, diamonds. When those jewelry boxes were opened the first yelp was from Debbie Allen, and like her, we each let out screams of surprise with awestruck emphasis. Yes, we were loud! Who would or could expect this kind of gift after all that had been given? I certainly could not have ever dreamed that this was coming. The diamond drop earrings that were given to each of the legends are deeee-vine, and the black-and-white diamond hoop earrings that each of the young'uns received are as beautiful.

Once that cherry was firmly on the top of that gigantic cake, we were taken back to the hotel to prepare for the actual ball. It was a black-and-white-themed ball, with the exception of our hostess, who wore red. The ballroom was exquisite, again the food was incredible, the music was provided by one of my favorites, trumpeter Chris Botti, and the reading again of "We Speak Your Names" was given—provoking again tears from us all. And from that moment, to use another song title, "Let's Get This Party Started" became the theme. And I must say, the girl knows how to throw a party.

We danced the night away with everybody joining in what became a jam session. Gladys Knight, Tina Turner, Patti LaBelle, Nancy Wilson, Valerie Simpson, and the list goes on, all became a part of the entertainment that went well into the morning hours. I, being one of the smart ones, looked at my watch and decided if I was going to get up in time for the Sunday brunch, I had better head for the door to my room, and I did.

The Sunday brunch was the absolute finishing touch to this spectacular weekend. Edwin Hawkins, Tremaine Hawkins, Walter Hawkins, and featured voices of their choir started the morning "service," and that is what we had, true Sunday morning service. BeBe Winans hosted the service and, as the singing became the focus as only BeBe can do, he started a song called "Changed," and once he left the stage and walked along the area that we were seated in, he passed the microphone first to "pastor" Shirley Caesar. And the service took on another level. He passed the microphone to me and I sang. Among those who were handed the microphone and sang their hearts out were Yolanda Adams, Gladys Knight, Chaka Khan, Patti LaBelle, Valerie Simpson, and it went on from there. It was spectacular.

Someone asked if something like this would be done for men. I don't remember who raised the question, but Mr. Poitier responded, saying, "I believe it already has, for we are the kind of men we are because of these kinds of women." That truly sanctions the saying "Behind every successful man is a woman."

Oprah said that the twenty-five women she had chosen were the ones she felt provided shoulders for her to stand on to reach her goals.

I remember saying to her, "Simply saying thank you would have been sufficient." And Oprah looked at me and said, "This is the way that I wanted to say thank you." I guess the lesson here is you never know who is watching you and learning from your actions.

The ride back to Los Angeles was full of remembering, or trying to remember, what just happened to me and the twenty-four other ladies. Even now, a thought will come to me about that weekend that makes me smile the biggest smile and say, "Wow!"

DIONNE'S LESSONS LEARNED

- *You never know who is watching you and learning from your actions.*

CHAPTER 18

————————

A House Is Not a Home

GROWING UP in a neighborhood that virtually resembled the United Nations gave me a head start in navigating the many different cultures that I have been exposed to over these years of world traveling. The changes to the area where I grew up are amazing. Sterling Street, the street that I grew up on, no longer exists. But the area is still a neighborhood of many nationalities.

I love being able to say that the friends I made throughout my growing years are still my friends. When I have more than an hour at home, I love to catch up on marriages, children, grandchildren, and what everyone is now doing: real fun stuff.

Some of my best friends from the neighborhood are Pat "Patsy" Munford, Joann "Jobie" Brownley, Elaine Chambers, Maxine Neal, Dougie and Lenny Munford, Karen Miller, Arlene Gregory, Carolyn De Paselena, Barbara Jones, Lorraine Miller, Leslie Uggams, and too many more to try to tax my brain. And my steady go-out gals are

Mikki Drinkard, Diane Mosely, Linda Hawkins, Roe Preston, and Shirley Hendricks.

Also, there is a wealth of talented people who come from my state of New Jersey, and the list is mind-boggling. I will name just a few to give you an idea of what I mean:

Count Basie; Sarah Vaughan; Cannonball and Nat Adderley; Kool and the Gang (and they still live there); the Isley Brothers; Melba Moore; John Amos; the current mayor of East Orange, Robert Bowser (I went to school with him); the newly inducted speaker of the state general assembly, Sheila Oliver (I went to school with her, too); Shirley Hendricks, an activist who writes a column in our local paper; Frank Sinatra; Lauryn Hill; Jerry Lewis; Ben Vereen; and, of course, my cousin Whitney Houston.

So yes, you betcha I'm proud to have been a part of this incredible state and I still reside in New Jersey. One of our neighborhood movie houses had the wonderful idea to create in front of the theater a Walk of Fame, which would let all who live there know about some of the people who also grew up there and went on to follow and obtain their dreams. Unfortunately, the theater is now closed, but our mayor thought to remove the engraved plaques and put them at the front walk of the new community performing arts school. Brilliant idea, if I say so myself.

I have no doubt that in the very near future on the Walk of Fame will be the next CEOs of major corporations; actors and actresses winning Academy Awards; musicians writing and scoring for film and Broadway shows; professors, physicians, and doctors specializing in every area of medicine; and others who are living their dreams. And I know they all will be as proud as I am to say that they are from neighborhoods throughout New Jersey. No matter how far I travel from home, I'll always be a "Jersey girl."

Brazil is my second home; I refer to it as my "stress-free country." I began touring more of this glorious country throughout the years. It was about eighteen years ago, after finishing an extensive tour, that I woke to watch the sunrise from my hotel balcony. I decided then that I was where I was supposed to be living. I called a friend and asked if he knew a real estate agent. Through his loud laughter he said, "Aha, we gotcha!" And I said yes.

That afternoon he and a real estate agent took me to look at several areas of Rio. I gave them just one prerequisite—I had to be able to see the large Christ the Redeemer statue, which was completed in 1931 and stands atop the Corcovado Mountain. I looked at several apartments, but since I am accustomed to living in a house, the apartments, although very nice, were not where I wanted to live. We finished the day without finding me a new home.

The next day, we started bright and early. This time the agent said that she had found the "perfect" place for me. Yep, she was absolutely right. The house she found was in the Jardin Botanico. The minute I entered the gates into the parking area, the first thing I saw was the Christ looking at me. I settled on the house and became a resident of Rio.

Living in Brazil, I found what I feel is missing here at home. These people openly embrace the values I was brought up with, such as the respect for elders, the absolute love of our country, the love of family, and the love of God—without fear of what others might think.

It was apparent that I had made the right decision. My friends there in Brazil all smile when I speak of Brazil with such reverence. I do because it is truly the way that I feel about the country. The wonderful people of Brazil have given me the biggest embrace, and I in turn have embraced them in the same manner.

I must confess that the beauty of the beaches is exactly as described in all of the travel brochures, miles and miles of white sand—which brings me to my confession. I am not a beach person; I don't like sand. You can never get rid of it. No matter how many showers you take, it will always be with you. The other thing is that I don't like things that crawl, scurry, or fly.

Yep, I am a complete "city girl," yet here I am surrounded by sand and things that crawl, scurry, and fly. I guess as long as I did not disturb those types of things and their habitats, I figured they would not disturb mine. And I have to say it has worked out perfectly over the years.

Learning to speak Portuguese, the language of the country, has been and still is the hardest part of living there. My Portuguese is very "suspect." I garner a lot of cocked heads and broad smiles as I try to speak. Somehow, I get my point across with a lot of hand language. I guess because I do sincerely try to communicate, the folks are understanding. I was told that I would learn the language through the music. Since I do sing in Portuguese and since I have to know and believe what I am saying in order to sing it, I have found that they were right on.

I feel truly blessed that I have found my paradise. As I get closer to the twilight years of my life, I know this is where I will be spending those years. When I get to the Brazilian portion of my show, I tell my audiences this is a "must visit" place. And many have told me that they have taken my advice and have visited Brazil. They now understand my love of the country. So the same invitation is now extended to you. Try it; I know you will like it.

CHAPTER 19

My Favorite Time of Year

I 'VE OFTEN said that I wish it could be Christmas year-round. It is the time of year when smiles, hugs, "hellos," holding doors open, helping with packages, and making contributions seem to take over everyone. Strangers greet you with "Merry Christmas" and a huge smile. I can definitely say Christmas is my most favorite time of year. The year always seems to rush along right after the Fourth of July. Before you know it, the rush to get out the decorations and start gift shopping is on us. I love all that goes with this holiday.

First and foremost, I know from my early teaching that this is a holy day in celebration of the birth of Jesus Christ. I have a practice of actually singing "Happy Birthday" to Him. I also say a prayer, being that I am thankful for His birth, and most certainly thankful for His willing to die so that I and all others can continue to enjoy life.

Christmas in our family is observed in a traditional, family-centered way, including friends. There is always the best of Christmas music being played either on the radio, the CD player, or live in my home. My home has become the family gathering place since my mommy and Aunt Rebie have passed, and it appears that I have been designated to continue on the tradition of chief cook and dishwasher, too.

This might be the only time of the year that I do cook, and yes, I prepare the entire meal. I put up my Christmas tree on my birthday, December 12, and from that day on, the tree is dressed at my leisure, so by the time Christmas Eve arrives it is completed.

I start preparing the meal the evening of the twenty-third and do the pastries first: apple and sweet potato pies, chocolate layer cake, coconut layer cake, and a pound cake. There are string beans, collard greens, cabbage, succotash, candied yams, macaroni and cheese, pepper rice, chicken and dumplings (my favorite), yeast rolls, glazed ham, roast chicken and turkey (both with corn bread dressing), leg of lamb, and a variety of drinks. (I'm making myself hungry.)

The only time I allow anyone in the kitchen with me is while I am making the pastries. My mommy and Aunt Rebie taught me that people in the kitchen while you are cooking are just in the way. I start the turkey and roast chickens on Christmas Eve just before I go to bed and let them cook through the night. (Did I say night? I usually am not ready to go to bed before three or four in the morning on Christmas Day.) The vegetables are started that evening, and the ham is put into the oven Christmas Day, as is the macaroni and cheese, and the rolls. I cook the hen for the chicken and dumplings on Christmas Eve, and make and cook the dumplings an hour before everyone is to show up.

I have also become the official gift wrapper. How I get myself into these extra-added activities I don't know. But because I am wrapping my gifts, I guess a few more to wrap is not too bad. Seeing the eyes of the children is my joy, and hearing them ooh and aah makes it all worthwhile. This year, 2010, will be the first year since moving back to New Jersey that I will do the outside of my home, and I plan to make it a true "winter wonderland."

People have wondered why it took me so long to record my very first Christmas CD. I didn't record one until 2004. I was asked by Tena Clark, who is now the CEO of her own record company, DMI Records, if I'd be interested in doing the project for her label. I was introduced to Tena by my sons during their teen years. Being that this was something that I had wanted to do for a very long time, I said yes, and we were set to record shortly after. The recording studio in Pasadena, California, is one of the most incredible that I've recorded in. It was a wonderful two weeks preparing for and choosing and recording the songs for the sessions, and working with the musicians. And what a group of musicians and singers it was: I did duets with Gladys Knight and BeBe Winans. Dave Koz lent his soulful sax sounds, and it all resulted in what I feel is a beautiful presentation of Christmas music.

There are a few standout songs that I'd like to speak about.

I recorded "Joy to the World" the way we sang it in church during our Christmas program with the total gospel treatment. "I Believe in Christmas" was written by BeBe Winans, with whom I performed it. It is a truly lovely song that expresses my feelings about this holiday. I had promised myself that I would probably never sing "Silver Bells" again as it was Pope John Paul II's favorite. He requested it each time I performed at the Christmas at the Vatican shows, and yet I included it so that I could send him the CD. I recorded "Have Yourself a Merry Little Christmas" with Gladys, and we did our vocals at her studio in Las Vegas. It took us all of ten minutes to lay down our vocals, so we spent the rest of our time together laughing and eating. "O Come, All Ye Faithful" was my daddy's favorite Christmas carol, and I did this in dedication to him. It was probably the hardest of the songs to get through because of the emotions it stirred in me. I could not do it more than those two takes.

Rhino Records reissued the CD in 2007 and I am looking forward to doing another one.

CHAPTER 20

New School

L IKE MANY millions of others, I became a regular viewer of *American Idol,* and I am impressed with those who went on to take the top prize on the show and launched great careers in the recording industry. So I was excited when during its fifth season in 2006, *American Idol* paid tribute to Bacharach, David, and Warwick. The songs covered forty-five years of recording history and were evidence of something I always said: Once a hit, always a hit. As some of the contestants were learning the songs in rehearsal, they remarked that the songs were not easy. I wasn't surprised. I found myself saying repeatedly to each of the contestants, "Think about the words before you open your mouths to sing. Try speaking the words, as if talking to someone who you have feelings for."

I think the contestants did a good job, and I must say the exposure that Burt and I received from appearing on this show was massive. To have very young people come up to me in the airport, or in a store, or just on the street, and say that they saw me on *Ameri-*

can Idol and ask what it was like to meet Paris (Bennett) or Taylor (Hicks) or Katharine (McPhee)—I thought was wonderful. And I for one am grateful for the advantage of being recognized by a much younger group of people.

American Idol did help a few younger people find the value of sitting in my audiences at my concerts, hearing very old songs, and giving these songs fresh meaning to these new ears listening. Kelly Clarkson, Ruben Studdard, and Fantasia Barrino all became a part of the J Records roster, where Clive Davis worked his magic in making each of them million-selling recording artists who have all gone on to heights well earned within the industry. I feel we are all being given a firsthand look at those who could potentially be the next icons of the music world.

I hope those who receive the ultimate prize of the fame and fortune that comes with winning the show are protected and are given good advice so as not to fall into the "too much too soon" trap.

American Idol reminds me of the past, watching *The Arthur Godfrey Show, The Ted Mack Amateur Hour*—on which Gladys Knight performed at the age of seven—*The Jackie Gleason Show,* and *Solid Gold.* This too was television that paved the way for emerging talent.

CHAPTER 21

Why I Sing

W HY WE Sing" is a song I heard many years ago by Kirk Franklin and his choir, the Family. I was on my way home when it came on the radio. It caught my attention to the point that I turned up the radio and pulled my car over to listen to it without distraction.

The words that were being sung and spoken touched me and made me realize that Mr. Franklin had coined many of the reasons why I sing.

From the first time I sang in public, to the time in the New York City studio to record this CD of gospel songs I grew up singing— this has all confirmed for me how blessed I am to have been given this wonderful gift of being able to sing.

Music has a way of lifting you out of the dumps. It makes you smile. It can even can make you sing—sometimes very loudly—and make you get up and dance, too. So music is and can be a healing agent.

• • •

HAVE JUST returned to my hotel suite from doing my show here in Holland. It's now two thirty in the morning for me, and here I am back on this laptop. I'll be leaving for Liverpool, England, at six in the morning to do two concerts for the Variety Club, and then on to Athens, Greece, and then back home to New Jersey, where I will have enough time to unpack and repack before I leave for Los Angeles.

In Los Angeles, I will perform a song that I recorded some time ago for the Starlight Children's Foundation. Doing these kinds of performances for foundations that help people in need gives me a great deal of pleasure because it is by using my God-given gift that I am helping a multitude of children and people, giving them hope and, in some cases, possibly even a better or a longer life.

This brings to mind my gospel CD that I recorded in 2008 appropriately titled *Why We Sing.* I just described where I will be performing these next few days—that is one of the reasons why I sing.

Edgar Bronfman Jr., CEO of Warner Music Group, gave me the opportunity to go into the studio and record it. He told me that he thought it had been too long—more than thirty years—since I had recorded gospel, and he thought that the time was right. He was absolutely right. He had only one request of me: that I would record "The Battle Hymn of the Republic." Since I also love this song, it was a reasonable request that I fulfilled.

Doing this CD gave me a chance to get together with some very special people within the gospel field, and we had us a high-spirited time in that studio in New York City. BeBe Winans, Percy Bady, Teddy "Teddy Bear" Harmon, and my son Damon all had a hand in the production. BeBe wrote songs for me and sang on one of the songs he wrote with me. And it was a joyous pleasure to have the choir from my church, New Hope Baptist Church, on the CD as well.

We had absolute "service" in that recording studio. I know we scared the engineer a bit, as he probably was a good little Catholic boy, and I know he had never seen anyone get caught up in the spirit to the point of dancing and shouting because the spirit of the Lord was riding high in that studio that night.

When I walked into the control room, his eyes were the size of saucers, and when he looked at me all he could say was, "Miss Warwick, are you okay?" This brought a smile to my face as I said through tears, "Yes, baby, I am okay."

We had to take a break because my choir was not finished thanking the Lord. You see, this is something that cannot be turned on and off.

Once everyone had calmed down, we went back in and finished the last two songs. One of my favorite songs that the Drinkards used to sing, "Rise, Shine, and Give God the Glory," got us revved up again and another break was in order.

"The Lord Is My Shepherd" happens to be my personal favorite. It is the Twenty-third Psalm put to music by my aunts Cissy and Annie, and it took us to yet another break because in the process of singing it, the tears continued to flow. This song for me is a spiritual experience that I cannot and will not try to explain.

Of course, I had to include my "debut" song, "Jesus Loves Me," and I am so happy that it has become a favorite of my youngest grandchild, Lealand. She told me it is her "very first favorite song forever, Grammy." (My grandchildren call me Grammy.) I let her know that it is my very first favorite song forever, too.

I can say that being a gospel singer has formed my ability to connect with a lyric, feel the meaning of the melody that surrounds a lyric, and deliver the passion needed to convey the message of a song to my audiences.

I can also say that along with my knowledge of music, gospel has trained me how to use variations of notes at those times when I am vocally challenged—a bit hoarse, or with a cold—but still have to do a performance.

Most gospel singers who have gone on to record popular music—Aretha Franklin, Mavis Staples, Gladys Knight, Patti LaBelle—and all those within the world of gospel recordings, such as BeBe and CeCe Winans, Donnie McClurkin, Yolanda Adams, and the Hawkins Family, will tell you that there is nothing in the world that can prepare you vocally or give an understanding of a lyric better than singing gospel.

The title song, "Why We Sing," is a duet with my sister, Dee Dee. Her presence and being featured on this song was, and will always be, a very special moment, unlike any that I had ever felt in a recording studio before. And I can say without a doubt there will never be that kind of a moment again. I have always loved Dee Dee's sound—rich and full of heart. When we stood on either side of the mic looking into each other's face while singing "Why We Sing," the total meaning of the song took ahold of both of us at the same time, and through tears we somehow were able to complete the song.

We stood in the booth holding each other for a very long time, laughing and sobbing in each other's arms. And when we finally went into the control room to listen to what we had just recorded, everybody in the room was wiping away tears. Listening to the playback of the take brought another wave of tears, and another break was needed. Even our good little Catholic boy engineer was crying. "I felt something that I cannot explain," he said. That is just the way the spirit of the Lord will touch you.

'M NOT the only one who was touched by Dee Dee, who was a wonderful person as well as a great recording and performing artist. People will come to me and speak with reverence about her talent and how they have her recordings and have been in her audiences when she performed. She is still loved and very much missed.

Again, she and I started out together doing a multitude of background singing sessions in the studios of New York. We worked with practically everyone who was recording during the late 1950s through 1964, when my career started to take off and I had to leave the Gospelaires. But Dee Dee continued to keep the group in great demand. Most of the background work we did together was for Jerry Leiber and Mike Stoller, Paul Case, Jerry Wexler, George Blackwell, Florence Greenberg—I guess you could say the industry as a whole. We sang behind the Drifters—all 69,000 versions of that group—Ben E. King, Chuck Jackson, Maxine Brown, and too many others for me to try to remember. Dee Dee and the group went on to record with Aretha Franklin before Aretha started to use the Sweet Inspirations and her sister's group. Aretha loved Dee Dee and the group's sound. The group also recorded with Van McCoy, Little Eva, Jackie DeShannon, and so many more. And of course, the group was on all of my recordings.

Dee Dee went on to record as a single artist and made some wonderful recordings. Before there was a Linda Ronstadt, my sister recorded "You're No Good" first. Before Diana Ross and the Supremes with the Temptations, my sister recorded "I'm Gonna Make You Love Me" first, for Mercury Records. Again, the promotion that every artist depended on, and which would have helped to put those recordings by Dee Dee into the mainstream, was lacking. And that isn't just my opinion; Dee Dee also felt that she didn't get the right support or promotion.

However, she did begin to have some success with recordings around 1965 with a song called "I Want to Be with You" and success with a song that happens to be my favorite of her recordings, "Foolish Fool." She was nominated for a Grammy with this recording and although she did not win it, she did win the hearts and ears of many. It appeared that she was on her way.

Looking back, however, I can see that Dee Dee honestly did not want to give up what has to be given to have a thriving career. She loved her privacy, and that is something that becomes a moot issue in this business. Also, she was a real "homebody," so traveling was not her favorite thing to do. She felt she was just not cut out to run around this world like her "crazy sister" does.

Dee Dee's last charted recordings were "She Didn't Know (She Kept On Talking)" and "Cold Nights in Georgia" in 1970, "Suspicious Minds" in 1971, and "Get Out of My Life" in 1975. Disappointed with the lack of promotion of these wonderful recordings, Dee Dee told me, "I'm going to leave the solo recording artist work to you."

In 1999 I proudly presented her with the Pioneer Award given to her by the Rhythm & Blues Foundation. It was a beautiful event held on the lot of MGM Studios in Los Angeles. I know it was a proud moment for her, but it was a prouder moment for my mommy and me.

Dee Dee had moved to Los Angeles but left for the same reason I did—that involuntary movement of the earth. She moved to Atlanta, Georgia, where she seemed to be very happy. It was during the time she lived in Georgia that her health began to fail and she thought it best to move back to New Jersey where I, Mommy, and all of our aunts and uncles were. She moved back into the home she grew up in with our mommy. It was a good move for her, as she was around those who loved and cared for her.

Around 2006, my son Damon was commissioned to produce and put together a recording date for the Tyler Perry film *Daddy's Little Girls* and record the song titled "Family First." Damon asked me if his idea to have our family sing this song was a good one, and I said I loved it. He then ran it by Tyler and Warner Bros. Records, and they loved the idea, too.

And there we all were: Cissy, Whitney, Gary, Bobbi Kris, Cheyenne, David, Kaelyn, Felicia, Dee Dee, and me. We went into the studio to record this wonderful song.

If you have not already, do yourself a favor and see *Daddy's Little Girls*. Tyler Perry and his team did a wonderful job telling the heartfelt story of a father's love for his daughters and what he goes through to raise them. Our song "Family First" plays at the very end over the credits.

Shortly after this project, I decided to put together a one-woman show and call it *My Music and Me* with hopes that it could possibly be of interest to Broadway. Who knows, I just might get lucky. I asked Dee Dee and my cousin Felicia if they wanted to go on the road with me when I did this show, as it was basically my life told through my music, with narrative by me. They both said they would, and the first place the show was performed was in London at the Shaw Theatre. To my great relief and joy, it was, and has since been, very well received.

Nothing made me prouder than being able to come back home and perform this show in South Orange, New Jersey, at the South Orange Performing Arts Center, a jewel box of a little theater. All of my friends and neighbors came out in support of me. And believe me, there are no bigger critics of my work. To paraphrase Sally Field, "They really liked me." Unfortunately, shortly after this performance and the recording session, Dee Dee began to experience serious health issues.

As fate would have it, the last time my sister and I sang alone was at the "Why We Sing" recording session.

Dee Dee and I were the best of friends. When she made her

transition on October 18, 2008, our family and the family of fans she had worldwide felt the void left in the music industry.

Dee Dee apparently reached far beyond just the music industry, as President Obama thought enough to send a wonderful letter of condolence on behalf of himself and the First Lady, Michelle.

For me, my sister will always live within my world.

HAVING BEEN born into a family of singers, I imagine you are wondering who else in the family might have had recording careers. Aside from recording with the Drinkard Singers, my aunt Cissy also recorded a few pop songs. And, for your information, she was the first to record "Midnight Train to Georgia" before Gladys Knight and the Pips. As with Dee Dee, the promotion on her recording was practically nil, so her record never really got much airplay.

Cissy has always been more like an older sister than an aunt. She lived with us until she married. We all walked to school together and, being the eldest of the kids, she was "sort of" in charge—which we did not like—until my mother got home from work. We all have always been close.

Cissy is now the matriarch of the family.

Her talent always speaks for itself. As the lead singer of the Sweet Inspirations, she traveled extensively with the group as well as with Elvis Presley and Aretha Franklin touring. Her voice can be heard on recordings doing background work with artists such as Aretha Franklin, Lou Rawls, Nina Simone, David Bowie, Luther Vandross, her daughter Whitney Houston, and her niece—me.

Professionally, she is known throughout the world, and not only has she had Grammy-nominated songs, but she won a Grammy for her gospel CD *Face to Face* in 1996. Cissy was honored by the Rhythm & Blues Foundation with the Pioneer Award in 1995.

She is still very much in demand and does several gospel festivals throughout the United States. And although her popularity is vast, she is best known as "Whitney's mother" and she loves it.

I am super proud of my family. They have been my strength, my support, and my guide throughout my career. And my strength, support, and guidance are given to them without hesitation.

We are unconditionally in love with each other.

And—we love to sing.

CHAPTER 22

Love, Laughter, and Losses

I HAVE BEEN asked a lot of questions, some of which were of the "duh" category and others that made me pause to think. Such was the question "How would I describe love?" Not to sound holier than thou, but I was taught "God Is Love."

Okay, now to get to what you really want me to address. I wish there was a word or a phrase that could describe love. Obviously, there are all of the well-known descriptions that I could fill this page with, but wouldn't you think, as I do, that love is an emotion that defies definition, given the many ways the word itself is used? For example: "I love the way you look." "I love the new dress." "I love the way you decorated the house." I could keep going forever.

Personally, I was "in love" with my husband, Bill, although I divorced him two weeks after we married and ended up remarrying him a year later. You see, my heart, where I heard love lives, won and from the second union we were blessed with two wonderful sons, and we were happy for the twelve years that followed. As with any relationship, be it with a girlfriend or boyfriend, engaged or married—all have those peaks and valleys. I had my share of both. Bill was a Gemini, whatever that means. I am a Sagittarius, again, whatever that means. We were supposed to be totally compatible. Well, we were for those twelve years, but then the foundation began to shift, making it difficult for the both of us to cope. The deep personal issue that drove us apart, I won't get into simply because it is none of your business. But I will say it was not a pleasant parting. However, it did give us both the freedom to move on, and that is exactly what we individually did.

During this time, I was recording for Warner Bros. and working with Thom Bell, a wonderful composer and producer, on an album project. I am saying that to say this: there are songs that can speak for you in any given situation. At this time, I was going through my divorce, and there were two particular songs I recorded that depicted the emotional ride I was on: "This House and Me" and "Once You Hit the Road." Singing them brought me through a few struggles during this time. This is why I know exactly what people mean when they tell me that a certain song of mine was able to strengthen them to face whatever they were going through.

I feel fortunate in that I can sing out my frustration, sadness, and happiness. To be able to sing "You looked inside my fantasies and made each one come true," or "You see this girl, this girl's in love with you," or "The look of love is on your face, a look that time can't erase." Come on, how lucky can I be? In the same breath sing, "Once you hit the road, baby, there ain't no turning back," or "What's it all about, Alfie? Is it just for the moment we live?" or "Don't make me over, accept me for what I am, accept me for the things that I do" or "Walk on by." They all give me words to let anyone know how I feel. So let music be your voice or set the mood you want to be in.

Music is also a wonderful preamble to getting intimate. Yes, I said intimate. Don't act like you don't know what I'm talking about. The music of Marvin Gaye, Barry White, and Isaac Hayes have all played very important parts in some of my most romantic, intimate moments. Hey—I know that's right.

I think my biggest mistake with those who have been a part of my personal life is that I fall in love before I fall in "like." Just like these lyrics:

My heart should be well schooled . . .

Now, the love for my children is totally unconditional, as is the love for my family. The love for my friends is heartfelt. My greatest love is my love for and of God.

Looking WAY back, I remember sitting one afternoon on my grandparents' porch. Their house was across the street from the city pool, and it was a very hot day in Camden, New Jersey. We wanted to go to the pool in the worst way, but Grandma said, "Maybe tomorrow," as she was having one of those mothers-of-the-church meetings and couldn't take us to the pool. Well, old smarty pants me, all of nine years old, decided that I was old enough to watch after my little sister. So I took Dee Dee by the hand and crossed the street to the pool entrance.

My first mistake was forgetting that the lifeguard and person who let you into the pool were both deacons at my grandfather's church.

My second mistake—well, I guess I don't have to tell you what happened when we were escorted back across the street by these two young men; I had never seen my grandmother so angry. Then the unexpected happened as I was prepared to die: she calmly told me to go up to my bedroom, wash up, and go to bed. It was only four o'clock in the afternoon. We had no air-conditioning and it was hot as the devil. But that's just what I did.

Around eight that night, she came into our bedroom and sat on the end of the bed. She asked why I had gone to the pool without permission, since she had just told me she would take Dee Dee and me the next day. I really didn't have an answer—except for how I felt when I grabbed Dee Dee by the hand and crossed that street. I felt I was old enough to take care of my little sister and myself.

Surprisingly, by the grace of God, this answer satisfied her. But leaving the front porch the way I did with my little sister in tow was what she was angry about. My grandmother ignored me for the next two days. She did not speak to me. She gave me no signs of even wanting me to be in her space. This was her way of punishing me and showing me (as we discussed much later in our lives) how much she loved me and cared about my well-being.

You see, crossing that street was being disrespectful and giving no regard to what my grandmother had said. She was waiting for, and got, an "I'm sorry and it will never happen again." And it never did.

Now, when Grandpa came up to our room, he wasn't a happy camper, either, but he wasn't as passive as Grandma was. He told me, in no uncertain terms, "If you ever even think to do something like that again . . ." He never finished the sentence. The next day, as promised, Grandma took Dee Dee and me to the pool, and although there was laughter, I knew I was still walking on thin ice and had to watch my p's and q's.

This story brings a smile to my face because it's an example of grandparents' love for their grandchildren. This kind of love is something that's not often talked about. However, it's the same kind of love I have for my grandchildren.

I love to smile; frowning is something I try to avoid. My grandpa told me when I was in one of my moods as a child that I should smile as often as I possibly could and I wouldn't get wrinkles. As I look in the mirror each day, I have to say my grandpa was absolutely right. Not one wrinkle to be seen.

I also love laughter. It's like music. It makes you feel good. It fills a room with a sound like none other. Laughter for me is the key to happy times. I'm sure you have been in a room where someone will start laughing and it became contagious, and before you knew it, everybody was laughing.

I laugh every chance I get. Some of the things I laugh at maybe I shouldn't. For instance, if I see you fall down, I will ask if you are okay but I'll be laughing. I just can't help myself.

A good joke will always make me laugh. But I am the pits when it comes to telling one. I will either laugh through it, knowing the punch line, or I have a tendency of sometimes forgetting the punch line. Most of the jokes I know that always get a laugh are visual, so you are all safe.

When I am in a grand funk, I turn to Abbott and Costello. They have a way of making me laugh and taking the mood of whatever I am going through out of my space on gales of laughter. The Three Stooges have that effect on me, too.

Life is serious enough to be taken seriously, as some people do. This can become boring, and it makes you boring.

A smile is something that I consider a gift. It is something that anyone can give to another without charge and it can change the feeling of an entire room full of people. The next time you are in a group of people, start smiling and watch the reaction of those in the room. Some might think you are crazy, but most will find it gives them a warm, fuzzy feeling. It's a feeling I happen to like a lot.

I think the best laugh anyone can have is when they are able to laugh at themselves. I laugh at me almost daily, and it has happened during my shows as well.

I have had the occasion of forgetting a lyric to a song and looking down into the first row to see somebody singing along with me and singing the right lyric, which takes me right to laughter. At the end of the song, I will let the folks know that I forgot the lyrics. It is very healthy to laugh, so do it as much as possible.

I have also said many times that I refuse to grow up. I remember how carefree childhood was for me. As I have gotten older, I realize that the reason for this is that grown-ups have too many problems. They frown a lot and all of them have wrinkles!

Now, there are things that will make me frown and be sad. Those are losses. Over these past few years, I have had to deal with many losses. My mother made her transition after dealing with a long illness. My sister made her transition a couple of years later; Dee Dee dealt with a severe case of rheumatoid arthritis. Believe me, I still deal with both of these losses daily.

Death is very selfish. It leaves those of us left behind to selfishly question reasons. Why should this happen, as we see it to be untimely? I know losing my mommy and my sister will always be great losses. But in my heart, when I think of them, I know they are both now without pain or stress and are in a better place.

I truly believe that there is a heaven and a hell. I know those who have had faith in God, as all of my family does, have been able to greet each other again. So I know my family is all together, keeping a watchful eye on the family members who are still here. To me, death is a transition.

I've also had the loss of some very dear friends and, again, have felt it was too soon for them to have made their transitions. When I got the news that Luther Vandross, one of my real buddies, had passed, it was as if a member of the family had passed.

The passing of Isaac Hayes, my big brother, was a shock, as I had spoken with him just two days before he passed. He sounded healthy and seemed to be recovering from his stroke.

Teddy Pendergrass: I just saw him at the Rhythm & Blues Foundation's gala in Philadelphia. He was so happy. Teddy looked great, and we took a picture, the last photo I would ever take with him. He also introduced me to Joan, his wife, who apparently put that beautiful smile he had on his face. I never would have thought looking at him that evening that he would be so close to leaving us.

Ted Kennedy. Although his health had not been the greatest for a while, you still just expect people like him to live forever. He was very dear to me, and I will miss him a great deal.

And my little "Mikey," Michael Jackson. The shock of all shocks. The last conversation I had with him was about how happy and excited he was about his upcoming tour. The song "Gone Too Soon" appropriately describes how I felt about Michael's transition.

I also lost my mentor, Lena Horne.

It's not easy dealing with the loss of a person who is dear to you. But then, Grandpa told me long ago that death is a part of life. Although I believe that, I still struggle with the finality of it.

And one other thing Grandpa told me: "You must not put a question mark where God puts a period."

F OR ME, having been brought up in a gospel-singing family and having a grandfather who was a minister, God has been and always will be a primary in my life. Going to church each Sunday from early morning through the evening was a way of life for all of us and is something I miss. My performance schedule prevents me from being at Sunday services, but Grandpa always told me that it is not the building called church, but that church is any-place that you feel you want to have your conversation with God. It could be, and has been, in my car, my bedroom, yes, even in my closet since I carry my church with me in my heart. So anywhere and anytime you feel the need to spend time with God is the right place and time to do so. My faith in God is a constant. I go no-where without knowing He is with me. I speak reverently of His existence, I continue to sing about Him, and the most important thing I constantly do is thank Him for being my guide, my refuge, my everything.

Explaining faith is not an easy thing to do because it is a very personal thing and everyone has that something that they feel is what keeps them going. The abovementioned happens to be my way.

My Wish

When the day comes (and it won't be for quite a while yet)
That I have made my transition
I think, and I say think, because I don't know,
I don't think anyone can say when that time will come,
But when it does, I hope that all that I have done over the years
I have prepared myself to know
The madness,
Pain (if any),
Accolades and
All that came with those years was done with pride and passion
And that I will be ready to greet those loved ones and friends
Who have gone on before me. In other words, as we say,
"I have put my house in order."

And I want all in attendance to do whatever my sons decide to do. Also, to be dressed in bright cheerful colors, and no crying will be allowed, since I won't be able to hear the sobs. I know I am going where I will have a *good* time, and that's what I want everybody to have, *a good time.*

I AM BEING constantly asked, "How do you want to be remembered?" I don't think there is an answer to that question. I hope I've done much too much to be remembered with *just a few words*!

DIONNE'S LESSON LEARNED

- *Don't fall in love before you fall in like.*

- *Laugh. Life is serious enough.*

- *Be respectful.*

- *Smile as often as possible.*

- *You must not put a question mark where God puts a period.*

- *Church is anyplace that you feel you want to have a conversation with God.*

CHAPTER 23

As I See It

THERE ARE still a few things that I hope to accomplish before I hang up my dancing shoes. I still have aspirations of working toward that Oscar, Emmy, and Tony. I will also be looking for that movie script, television show, and Broadway play that will give me the opportunity at least to try to give performances worthy of receiving those "rewards."

Your dreams are the first step to being, doing, and getting what it is that you want out of life.

My mantra, "If you can think it, you can do it," has been the truth throughout my life—from that magic moment the first time, at six years old, I sang "Jesus Loves Me" in public at my grandfather's church, until this very day.

At sixty-nine years young, I am still up at the crack of dawn to make a flight to who knows where. This continues until I get home, where I would hope to try to let the sun come up before me. But it just is not in the hand I have been dealt. So I just keep on doing what I do the way that I do it.

I'm sure we have all said at one time or another, "If I only knew then what I know now." I am no different. However, I don't think I would do anything differently, aside from keeping a sharper eye on the record companies I have recorded for. How much was I really due with regard to my record sales and royalties from those companies? I still don't know.

Other than that, I think the ups and downs that I have had so far have been a good thing. I feel I have grown stronger with each bump in the road. Now I know how to brace myself if I see another bump coming.

My Life, as I See It: I am healthy, happy, and truly blessed!

DIONNE'S LESSONS LEARNED

- *The truth prevails.*

A "Thank You" from
Dionne to Her Friends (Fans)

To ALL my friends around the world:

I feel truly blessed in that those whom I refer to as friends (fans) were "color-blind." They did not seem to notice that I was African American. I was and still am the artist singing the songs that they had grown to love and wanted to hear.

A huge thank-you goes out to all who were in my audiences at some point and those who purchased any of my recordings over these past fifty years.

Thanks for appreciating me not only for who I am, but for what I brought to you through my music.

When my music became popular throughout foreign lands such as France, England, Asia, Australia, Africa, Italy, Russia, Japan, the Arab Nations, and other parts of the world, it was a wonderful thing to experience. And, of course, I must include all of these regions when I say thank you for being supportive of my career for all of these wonderful years, without faltering.

Your loyalty to me through the hits and the dry periods when I had no new recordings on the market is very much appreciated.

Being one of the first in my peer group to travel throughout Europe and other continents gave me much to share with my friends and family, and for this, I am grateful. It has been quite an education for me as well, and one that will be with me eternally.

Thank you, friends!

Love,

Dionne

Dionne Warwick

MY LIFE, AS I SEE IT

50 LESSONS LEARNED

1. Remove "can't" from your vocabulary. As Grandpa told me, "If you can think it, you can do it!"

2. Establish a strong spiritual foundation. This will help sustain you through life's peaks and valleys.

3. It's never too late to pursue a passion. Do what makes you happy.

4. Encourage children to follow their dreams. Let them reach for the stars, and let them know you'll be there no matter what.

5. Create a support mechanism. Family is extremely important.

6. Success is unpredictable, so remember that patience truly is a virtue.

7. Always have a backup plan.

8. Hold your ground; don't compromise.

9. Establish a mentor relationship with someone experienced in the area you are interested in pursuing.

10. Learn to distinguish constructive criticism from destructive criticism; be receptive to constructive criticism, as it may be helpful to your career.

11. Be and let be.

12. Love can be elusive.

13. Always be honest. (Find someone you can trust.)

14. Change is caused by circumstances.

15. Be prepared.

16. Follow your dreams; dedication will see you through.

17. True friendship never really ends.

18. A lull in employment can be a period of personal growth.

19. Nothing beats a failure but a try.

20. It's never too late to be a student.

21. Being the best ain't such a bad thing.

22. You can't judge a book by its cover.

23. We are put here for the purpose of being of service to one another.

24. Caring and giving of time are the most precious things one can give another.

25. There but for the grace of God go I.

26. In battle, it's always primary to know what and whom you are fighting. Education is essential.

27. Show business is all about timing.

28. Children come first, adult relationships second.

29. Share responsibility in a relationship.

30. Don't let your children wake up to an "early morning stranger."

31. In a relationship, don't lose sight of *we, you,* and *ours.*

32. Mind your own business.

33. Age is just a number.

34. Your mind is the strongest part of your body.

35. Success will dissipate over time.

36. Perfect the craft of giving audiences more than what is expected of you.

37. Think of yourself as a brand.

38. Dress, speak, and walk with swagger.

39. Believe that you can and you are.

40. Be humble and be consistent.

41. Our children are mirror images of ourselves.

42. It's important to have God in the lives of children.

43. You never know who is watching you and learning from your actions.

44. Don't fall in love before you fall in like.

45. Laugh. Life is serious enough.

46. Be respectful.

47. Smile as often as possible.

48. You must not put a question mark where God puts a period.

49. Church is anyplace that you feel you want to have a conversation with God.

50. The truth prevails.

Acknowledgments

FROM DIONNE WARWICK

THERE IS no way that this book could have been written without the complete support of quite a few people, and they are:

First and foremost, God for giving me the ability to remember that far back in my life, and career stories that I thought I had forgotten.

My wonderful sons David and Damon, and all my grandchildren: Cheyenne, Lealand, Kaelyn, Neko, Mandela, and Maya.

My family, for giving me the upbringing instilling dignity, hope, happiness, love, and that huge amount of encouragement. My friends, for being my friends, and all of my extended friends, those you might call fans.

Dave Wooley, what can I say? *Thank you* do not seem to be the most adequate words to use. But for lack of better words, I say "thank you" for your tenacity, thoroughness, for jarring my memory with the "right" questions, for your expertise and unlimited knowledge you so generously shared with me, for all of the sleepless nights you spent editing and putting my thoughts in proper order. Also, I have to thank your daughters for allowing their daddy to let me take so much of his time when I know he really wanted to be with both of you. But most of all, Dave, I thank you for believing that your "friend" (me) could do this!

The publishing team, Judith Curr and Malaika Adero, for believing there was a story in me to share and for allowing me to tell it my way.

David Vance, for making me look so amazing in the photo. He has a wonderful way of doing this and has for many years.

Al Hunter Jr., thanks for your dedication and support for this project.

Special thanks to Burt Bacharach and Hal David. Thank you, Burt, for putting those wonderful melodies to the incredible words of Hal David. And thank you, Hal, for those incredible words that I was able to utilize in many of the descriptions in the book.

Thanks to my manager, agents, business associates, and office staff.

A very special thanks to: Henry Carr, Marcella Kingi, Vivian Anderson, Beverly Todd, Kevin Sasaki.

My awesome musicians: Kathy Rubbicco, piano and conductor; Todd Hunter, keyboards; Rob Shrock, keyboards; Renato Brasa, percussion; Jeffrey Lewis, drums; Ernest Tibbs, bass.

My wonderful team: David Krause, travel and merchandise manager; Tony Carr, Ellis McBurrows, Barbara Simpson, Neil Barr, Carlos Keyes, Red Entertainment Agency; Debbie Fowler, light design; Deanna Warrick, road manager; Barry Warrick, sound engineer.

I also have to thank all of the wonderful people who have worked with me over the years. You know who you are.

My grandpa, thanks for giving me the courage to continue to believe "If you can think it, you can do it."

Last, but by no stretch of the imagination least, I want to thank "myself." Yes, you read that correctly, I said I want to thank myself.

I thank me for being able to remember all that I did, for using all of the skills of typing that I learned in high school, for staying true to the task of meeting the deadlines I set for myself. Also for staying up late into the night after my shows in front of this HP laptop computer (thanks, Hewlett-Packard), and most of all for being able to deliver what I hope will inspire, encourage, and be able to provide a few pieces of useful information.

—Dionne

Acknowledgments

FROM DAVID FREEMAN WOOLEY

FIRST AND foremost, I give thanks to God for all of my blessings.

My sincere love and thanks to my mother, Bettye Wooley St. John, and my beloved father, Herman J. Wooley, for being my parents. A special thanks to Harry St. John Jr. for your boundless support. Sincere thanks to Carol "Oma" Hopkins.

To my siblings Dwayne, Pierre, Terrance, and Tamani, as well as the entire Wooley family: I thank you all for your unconditional love and support. "We are family."

Thanks and gratitude to my loved ones and friends for your patience and encouragement while I was in the "trenches" working on this book. My gratitude and thanks to Al Hunter Jr. I am also grateful and indebted to my lifelong friends and mentors for sharing your wisdom with me. My thanks to the wonderful schools I attended: Holy Name School (New York City), Rice High School (Harlem, New York), University of Delaware, and Wilmington University (Delaware).

A big thank-you to the entire awesome team at Atria Books/ Simon & Schuster: Judith Curr, our wonderful publisher, thanks for believing in this book from Day One. Malaika Adero, editor extraordinaire, thanks for your honesty, commitment, guidance, and also for believing in this book from Day One. Thanks to Todd Hunter for all you do.

Ms. Dionne Warwick, or as I call you, "D," I would like to express my sincere and profound thanks to you for our twenty-plus years of true friendship. It's been an honor and a privilege to call you my friend. As my business partner, your acumen is second to none. Collaborating with you on this book has been an amazing journey, with blessings every step of the way. This experience is one I will forever treasure. "D," there have been many words said and written to describe you. However, for me, it simply comes down to one word: *Genius*.

Finally, a love-filled thanks to my wonderful daughters, Veda Davida and Davina E'man Wooley. You're my two heartbeats and a constant source of love and inspiration. Something for you, as well as the future generations of the Wooley family, to remember always: pursue your dreams with passion and purpose in an effort to achieve perfection. I'm so very proud of you both. I love you.—Daddy

May God bless you all—Dave Wooley

"We Are the World"

(FROM "HEARTBREAKER," CHAPTER 5)

Writers: Michael Jackson and Lionel Richie
Conductor: Quincy Jones
Recorded: 1985

Soloists (in order of appearance):

Lionel Richie	Al Jarreau
Stevie Wonder	Bruce Springsteen
Paul Simon	Kenny Loggins
Kenny Rogers	Steve Perry
James Ingram	Daryl Hall
Tina Turner	Huey Lewis
Billy Joel	Cyndi Lauper
Michael Jackson	Kim Carnes
Diana Ross	Bob Dylan
Dionne Warwick	Ray Charles
Willie Nelson	

Chorus:

Dan Aykroyd, Harry Belafonte, Lindsey Buckingham, Mario Cipollina, Johnny Colla, Sheila E., Bob Geldof, Bill Gibson, Chris Hayes, Sean Hopper, Jackie Jackson, La Toya Jackson, Marlon Jackson, Randy Jackson, Tito Jackson, Waylon Jennings, Bette Midler, John Oates, Jeffrey Osborne, Anita Pointer, June Pointer, Ruth Pointer, and Smokey Robinson.

The "Legends" and the "Young'uns"

HONORED BY OPRAH WINFREY

(FROM "AWARDS/REWARDS AND THE
LEGENDS BALL," CHAPTER 17)

The Legends:

Maya Angelou, Shirley Caesar, Diahann Carroll, Elizabeth Catlett, Ruby Dee, Katherine Dunham, Roberta Flack, Aretha Franklin, Nikki Giovanni, Dorothy Height, Lena Horne, Coretta Scott King, Gladys Knight, Patti LaBelle, Melba Moore, Toni Morrison, Rosa Parks, Leontyne Price, Della Reese, Diana Ross, Naomi Sims, Tina Turner, Cicely Tyson, Alice Walker, Dionne Warwick, and Nancy Wilson.

The Young'uns:

Yolanda Adams, Debbie Allen, Ashanti, Tyra Banks, Angela Bassett, Kathleen Battle, Halle Berry, Mary J. Blige, Brandy, Naomi Campbell, Mariah Carey, Pearl Cleage, Natalie Cole, Kimberly Elise, Missy Elliott, Pam Grier, Iman, Janet Jackson, Judith Jamison, Beverly Johnson, Alicia Keys, Chaka Khan, Audra McDonald, Terry McMillan, Suzan-Lori Parks, Phylicia Rashad, Valerie Simpson, Anna Deavere Smith, and Alfre Woodard.

Dionne Warwick Grammy History

Dionne Warwick has been nominated for
thirteen Grammy Awards and has won five.
The New York Chapter of NARAS (National Academy of
Recording Arts and Sciences) has awarded Dionne Warwick,
Burt Bacharach, and Hal David with the Heroes Award.

Grammy Wins

1968: Best Contemporary Pop Vocal Performance, Female, "Do You Know the Way to San Jose." (Dionne Warwick was the first African American artist to win since Ella Fitzgerald.)

1970: Best Contemporary Vocal Performance, Female, "I'll Never Fall in Love Again"

1979: Best Pop Vocal Performance, Female, "I'll Never Love This Way Again"

1979: Best R&B Vocal Performance, Female, "Déjà Vu." (Dionne Warwick was the first female solo artist to win Grammy awards in pop and R&B in the same year.)

1986: Best Pop Performance by a Duo or Group with Vocal, "That's What Friends Are For" (with Elton John, Gladys Knight, Stevie Wonder)

Grammy Nominations

1964: Best Rhythm and Blues Recording, "Walk On By"

1967: Best Contemporary Solo Vocal Performance, Female, "I Say a Little Prayer"

1967: Best Vocal Performance, Female, "Alfie"

1969: Best Contemporary Vocal Performance, Female, "This Girl's in Love with You"

1974: Best Pop Vocal Performance by a Duo or Group, "Then Came You" (with the Spinners)

1985: Record of the Year, "That's What Friends Are For"

1985: Best Pop Vocal Performance, Female, "Friends"

1991: Best R&B Performance by a Duo or Group with Vocals, "Superwoman" (with Gladys Knight and Patti LaBelle)

Dionne Warwick
Honorary Doctorate Awards

Honorary Doctorate Degree, Hartt College
Honorary Doctorate Degree, Bethune-Cookman University
Honorary Doctorate Degree, Shaw University
Honorary Doctorate Degree, American Bar Association
Honorary Doctorate Degree, Columbia College of Chicago
Honorary Doctorate Degree, Lincoln College
Honorary Doctorate Degree, University of Maryland Eastern Shore

Dionne Warwick
Selected Singles Discography

Scepter

1962: "Don't Make Me Over"/"I Smiled Yesterday"

1962: "Don't Make Me Over"/"Make the Music Play," "I Smiled Yesterday"/"Wishin' and Hopin' " (France)

1963: "This Empty Place"/"Wishin' and Hopin' "

1963: "This Empty Place"/"I Cry Alone," "It's Love That Really Counts"/"Make It Easy on Yourself" (France)

1963: "Make the Music Play"/"Please Make Him Love Me"

1964: "Walk On By"/"Any Old Time of Day"

1964: "Walk On By"/"Put Yourself in My Place," "I Could Make You Love Me"/"Shall I Tell Her" (France)

1964: "A House Is Not a Home"/"You'll Never Get to Heaven"

1964: "Reach Out for Me"/"How Many Days of Sadness"

1965: "Who Can I Turn To"/"Don't Say I Didn't Tell You So"

1965: "You Can Have Him"/"Wives and Lovers," "Don't Say I Didn't Tell You So"/"Only the Strong, Only the Brave" (France)

1965: "Here I Am"/"Close to You"

1965: "Looking with My Eyes"/"Only the Strong, Only the Brave"

1965: "Are You There with Another Girl"/"If I Ever Make You Cry"

1966: "Message to Michael"/"Here Where There Is Love"

1966: "Trains and Boats and Planes"/"Don't Go Breaking My Heart"

1966: "I Just Don't Know What to Do with Myself"/"In Between the Heartaches"

1966: "Another Night"/"Go with Love"

1966: "Oh Yeah Yeah Yeah" (with Sacha Distel, live)/"What'd I Say (live), "Don't Go Breaking My Heart"/"In Between the Heartaches" (France)

1967: "Alfie"/"The Beginning of Loneliness"

1967: "The Windows of the World"/"Walk Little Dolly"

1967: "I Say a Little Prayer"/"(Theme from) Valley of the Dolls"

1968: "Do You Know the Way to San Jose"/"Let Me Be Lonely"

1968: "There's Always Something There to Remind Me"/"Who's Gonna Love Me"

1968: "Promises, Promises"/"Whoever You Are I Love You"

1968: "This Girl's in Love with You"/"Dream Sweet Dreamer"

1969: "The April Fools"/"Slaves"

1969: "Odds and Ends"/"As Long as There's an Apple Tree"

1969: "You've Lost That Lovin' Feeling"/"Window Wishing"

1970: "I'll Never Fall in Love Again"/"What the World Needs Now Is Love"

1970: "Let Me Go to Him"/"Loneliness Remembers What Happiness Forgets"

1970: "My Way"/"Something" (France)

1970: "Paper Mache"/"The Wine Is Young"

1970: "Make It Easy on Yourself" (live)/"Knowing When to Leave"

1970: "The Green Grass Starts to Grow"/"They Don't Give Medals to Yesterday's Heroes"

1971: "Who Gets the Guy"/"Walk the Way You Talk"

1971: "Amanda"/"He's Moving On"

1971: "The Love of My Man"/"Hurts So Bad"

1972: "Raindrops Keep Falling on My Head"/"Is There Another Way to Love You"

1972: "I'm Your Puppet"/"Don't Make Me Over"

1972: "Reach Out and Touch"/"All Kinds of People"/"The Good Life"

Warner Bros.

1972: "If We Only Have Love"/"Close to You"

1973: "I'm Just Being Myself/"You're Gonna Need Me"

1973: "Don't Let My Teardrops Bother You"/"I Think You Need Love"

1974: "Then Came You"/"Just As Long as We Have Love" (with the Spinners)

1974: "Sure Thing"/"Who Knows"

1975: "Take It from Me"/"It's Magic"

1975: "Once You Hit the Road"/"World of My Dreams"

1975: "Once You Hit the Road" (12-inch)/"Once You Hit the Road" (instrumental)

1976: "His House and Me"/"Ronnie Lee"

1976: "I Didn't Mean to Love You"/"He's Not for You"

ABC

1977: "By the Time I Get to Phoenix"/"I Say a Little Prayer"/"That's the Way I Like It" (with Isaac Hayes, live)

Warner Bros.

1977: "Do You Believe in Love at First Sight"/"Do I Have to Cry"

1977: "Keepin' My Head Above Water"/"Livin' It Up Is Startin' to Get Me Down"

Musicor

1977: "If I Ruled the World"/"Only Love Can Break a Heart"

Warner Bros.

1978: "Don't Ever Take Your Love Away"/"Do I Have to Cry"

1978: "I Didn't Mean to Love You" (full version)/"I Didn't Mean to Love You" (instrumental)

Arista

1979: "I'll Never Love This Way Again"/"In Your Eyes"

1979: "Déjà Vu"/"All the Time"

1980: "After You"/"Out of My Hands"

1980: "Feeling Old Feelings" (winner Tokyo music prize)/"The Letter"

1980: "No Night So Long"/"Reaching for the Sky"

1980: "Easy Love"/"We Never Said Goodbye"

1981: "Some Changes Are for Good"/"This Time Is Ours"

1981: "There's a Long Road Ahead of Us"/live medley of hits

1982: "Friends in Love" (with Johnny Mathis)/"What Is This"

1982: "For You"/"With a Touch"

Geffen

1982: "State of Independence" (all-star choir)

Arista

1982: "Heartbreaker"/"I Can't See Anything (But You)"

1982: "All the Love in the World"/"It Makes No Difference Now" (France)

1983: "Take the Short Way Home"/"Just One More Night"

1983: "Yours"/"Take the Short Way Home" (UK)

1983: "All the Love in the World"/"You Are My Love"

1983: "How Many Times Can We Say Goodbye" (with Luther Vandross)/"I Do It 'Cause I Like It" (UK)

1983: "How Many Times Can We Say Goodbye" (with Luther Vandross)/"What Can a Miracle Do"

1983: "Got a Date" (12-inch)/"Got a Date" (instrumental)

1984: "Got a Date"/"Two Ships Passing in the Night"

1984: "Finder of Lost Loves" (with Glenn Jones)/"It's Love"

Columbia

1984: "We Are the World" (all-star choir)

Arista

1985: "Run to Me" (with Barry Manilow)/"Heartbreaker"/"Paradise Café"

(Barry Manilow) (UK)

1985: "Run to Me" (with Barry Manilow)/"No Love in Sight" (Barry Manilow)

1985: "That's What Friends Are For" (with Elton John, Gladys Knight, and Stevie Wonder)/"Two Ships Passing in the Night"

1986: "Whisper in the Dark"/"Extravagant Gestures"

1987: "Love Power" (with Jeffrey Osborne, promo)

1987: "Love Power" (with Jeffrey Osborne)/"In a World Such as This"

1987: "Love Power (Energy of Love)" (with Jeffrey Osborne)/"In a World Such as This"

1987: "Reservations for Two" (with Kashif)/"For Everything You Are"

1987: "For Everything You Are" (perfume promo single)

1987: "Another Chance to Love" (with Howard Hewett)/"Cry on Me"

Motown

1989: "Forgotten Eyes" (with Singers for Sight)

Arista

1989: "Heartbreaker/"I Can't See Anything But You"/"All the Love in the World"/"You Are My Love" (3-inch, UK)

1989: "The Promise of Life" (for SIDS charity)

1989: "Take Good Care of You and Me" (promo)

1989: "Take Good Care of You and Me" (with Jeffrey Osborne)/"Heartbreak of Love" (with June Pointer)

1990: "Take Good Care of You and Me"/"Heartbreaker"/"Love Power" (UK)

1990: "Walk Away"/"A True Love" (with Sacha Distel)/"All the Love in the World" (UK)

1990: "I Don't Need Another Lover" (with the Spinners, 2 mixes, promo)

1990: "I Don't Need Another Lover" (with the Spinners)/"Heartbreaker"

Epic

1990: "Lift Every Voice and Sing" (charity single)

BMG

1991: Blue System, "It's All Over" (with Dieter Bohlen)

1993: "Friends Can Be Lovers" (different rhythm track)/"Fragile"/ "Will You Still Love Me Tomorrow" (Germany)

Arista

1993: "Sunny Weather Lover" (promo)

1993: "Sunny Weather Lover"/"I Sing at Dawn" (3-inch, Japan)

1993: "Sunny Weather Lover"/" 'Til the End of Time"

1993: "Where My Lips Have Been"/"Fragile"

1993: "Friends Can Be Lovers"/"Age of Miracles"

1994: "A Taste of Brazil" (Jobim medley)/"Virou Areia"/"Oh Bahia"/ "Captives of the Heart" (promo)

1994: "Captives of the Heart"/"10,000 Words" (promo)

Polydor

1995: "Just Like a Woman" (with Grace Bumbry)

Sin Drome Records

1996: "Sweet Praline (When You're So Far Away)" (with Jazz Crusaders)

Wave Entertainment

1997: "If I Let Myself Go" (with Chuck Jackson)/"I'll Never Get Over You" (Chuck Jackson)

River North

1998: "Walk On By" (promo)

1998: "What the World Needs Now" (with the Hip-Hop Nation United, 5 mixes)

1998: "I Promise You" (promo)

Alta Tensione

2001: "Think About Me" (with the Royal Philharmonic Orchestra)

Tommy Boy Records

2001: "We Are Family" (all-star choir)

Arista

2003: "I Don't Need Another Love" (8 mixes, promo)

Arista

2003: "I Don't Need Another Love" (with the Spinners, 3 mixes)

Warner Bros.

2003: "What Goes Around" (with Jools Holland and His Rhythm and Blues Orchestra)

Sony Italy

2005: "It's Forever" (with Mariella Nava)

Concord Records

2007: "Close to You" (with Mya)

Rhino Records

2008: "I'm Going Up" (featuring BeBe Winans, promo)

2008: *Why We Sing* (radio sampler) "Show Me the Way"/"With All My Heart"/"I'm Going Up"

Dionne Warwick Selected Album Discography

Scepter Records

1963: *Presenting Dionne Warwick*

1964: *Anyone Who Had a Heart*

1964: *Make Way for Dionne Warwick*

1965: *The Sensitive Sound of Dionne Warwick*

1965: *Here I Am*

1966: *Dionne Warwick in Paris* (live)

1966: *Here Where There Is Love*

1967: *On Stage and in the Movies*

1967: *The Windows of the World*

1967: *Golden Hits,* part 1

1968: *The Magic of Believing* (gospel)

1968: *Valley of the Dolls*

1968: *Promises, Promises*

1969: *Soulful*

1969: *Greatest Motion Picture Hits*

1969: *Golden Hits,* part 2

1970: *I'll Never Fall in Love Again*

1970: *Very Dionne*

1971: *The Love Machine*

1971: *Dionne Warwick Story: A Decade of Gold* (live)

1972: *From Within*

Warner Bros.

1972: *Dionne*

1973: *Just Being Myself*

1975: *Then Came You*

1975: *Track of the Cat*

ABC Records

1977: *A Man and a Woman* (with Isaac Hayes, live)

Warner

1977: *Love at First Sight*

Arista

1979: *Dionne*

1980: *No Night So Long*

1981: *Hot! Live and Otherwise* (live)

1982: *Friends in Love*

1982: *Heartbreaker*

1983: *Dionne: The Collection* (UK)

1983: *How Many Times Can We Say Goodbye* (US), aka *So Amazing* (UK)

1985: *Finder of Lost Loves* (US), aka *Without Your Love* (UK)

1985: *Friends*

1987: *Reservations for Two*

1989: *Love Songs* (UK)

1989: *Greatest Hits 1979–1990*

1989: *Greatest Hits 1979–1990* (Europe, different track listing)

1990: *Dionne Warwick Sings Cole Porter*

1990: *Dionne Warwick Sings Cole Porter* (Japan, bonus track)

1993: *Friends Can Be Lovers*

1994: *Aquarela do Brasil* (Water Colors of Brazil)

Sony Classical

1994: *Celebration in Vienna* (with Plácido Domingo, live)

River North

1998: *Dionne Sings Dionne*

Victor Entertainment

2000: *Dionne Sings Dionne 2*

DMI

2004: *My Favorite Time of the Year* (holiday)

Concord Records

2007: *My Friends and Me*

Rhino Records

2008: *Why We Sing* (gospel)

Dionne Warwick
Foreign Language Selected Discography

Italian

1964: "Apro Gil Occhi" (A House Is Not a Home)

1964: "Non Mi Pentiro" (Walk On By)

1967: "La Vita Come Va" (The Windows of the World)

1967: "Ogni Donna Che Amerai" (Walk Little Dolly)

1967: "Dedicato all'amore" (For the Rest of My Life)

1967: "La Voce del Silenzio" (Silent Voices) (winner San Remo Song Festival)

German

1964: "Geh Vorbei" (Walk On By)

1964: "Ich Warte Jeden Tag" (You'll Never Get to Heaven)

French

1966: "You'll Never Get to Heaven" (live)

1966: "A House Is Not a Home" (live)

1966: "O Yeah Yeah Yeah" (with Sacha Distel, live)

1966: "The Good Life" (live)

1966: "La Vie en Rose" (live)

1966: "La Vie en Rose" (studio)

1964: "Un Toit Ne Suffit Pas" (A House Is Not a Home)

1998: "Si l'On Pouvait Arrêter le Temps" (If We Could Stop Time) (with Sacha Distel)

Spanish

1997: "Si Me Dejo Llevar" (If I Let Myself Go) (with Chuck Jackson)

Portuguese

1992: "Quase Um Sonho" (Almost a Dream) (with Jose Augusto)

1993: "Camaleao"

1994: "Jobim Medley"

1994: "Virou Areia"

1994: "Oh Bahia"

1994: "Piano Na Mangueira" (with Chico Buarque)

1994: "Samba Dobrado"

1994: "Heart of Brazil" (with Eliana Estevao)

1994: "N'Kosi Sikelel'i—Afrika"/"So Bashiya Bahlala Ekhaya"

1994: "Brazil" (Aquarela do Brasil) (part 1)

1994: "Flower of Bahia" (with Dori Caymmi)

1998: "Brazil" (Aquarela do Brasil) (part 2)

2002: "Song of Ossanha"

2002: "Lua Candeia" (Moonlight)

2007: *Live at Via Funchal, São Paulo, Brasil* (for an upcoming CD/ DVD release)

> with Gilberto Gil: "Sarara Crioulo"
>
> with Jorge Benjor: "Mas Que Nada"
>
> with Ivan Lins: "She Walks This Earth"
>
> with Simone and Ivan Lins: "Comecar de Novo"
>
> with Emilio Santiago: "Aquarela do Brasil" (Water Colors of Brazil)
>
> with Batacoto: "Virou Areia"
>
> with Milton Nascimento: "Travessia" (in studio)

Dionne Warwick
Selected Guest Appearance
Discography

1963: *Memories of the Cow Palace,* "Don't Make Me Over" (live)

1964: *The Greatest on Stage,* "What'd I Say"/"Anyone Who Had a Heart" (live)

1965: *What's New Pussycat* original soundtrack, "Here I Am"

1965: *Murray the K's Greatest Holiday Show,* "Walk On By/"Reach Out for Me" (live)

1967: *Valley of the Dolls* original soundtrack, "(Theme from) Valley of the Dolls"

1969: *Slaves* original soundtrack, "Slaves"

1971: *Love Machine* original soundtrack, "He's Moving On" and "Amanda" from film, and includes pop versions produced by Burt Bacharach and Hal David

1975: Spinners, *Pick of the Litter,* "Just As Long As We Have Love" (with the Spinners)

1977: *Gut Gestimmt, Stars Im Studio,* "Feelings" and "Love to Love You Baby" (with the SFB Big Band live)

1977: *Love at First Sight,* "Love at First Sight"

1980: *Television's Greatest Hits '70s and '80s,* "Solid Gold Theme" (part 1)

1981: *Jacqueline Susann's Valley of the Dolls,* "What Becomes of Love"

1981: *Tom Jones Show Greatest Hits,* "Endless Love" (with Tom Jones) and "There's a Long Road Ahead of Us" (live)

1981: *World Song Festival '81,* Bobby Vinton and Dionne Warwick (live)

1982: *Donna Summer,* "State of Independence"

1983: *The Jigsaw Man* (TV show), "Only You and I"

1984: *The Woman in Red* original soundtrack, "It's You" and "Weakness" (with Stevie Wonder), "Moments Aren't Moments"

1984: Winter Olympics Theme, "Just a Dream Away"

1985: USA for Africa, "We Are the World"

1985: Westwood One Radio live recording, also released as Budweiser Concert series LP, includes a dynamite version of "Touch Me in the Morning" (live)

1985: *Tube Tunes, Vol. 3: The '80s,* "Love Boat Theme"

1985: "Solid Gold Theme" (part 2)

1986: *The Seduction* (TV show), "Love's Hiding Place"

1986: *Motown . . . Fame . . . & Beyond,* "Starlight"

1986: *Dave Clark's Time,* "What on Earth" and "Within My World"

1987: Richard Carpenter, *Time,* "In Love Alone"

1987: *Woman to Woman* theme song

1988: Johnny Mathis, *Once in a While,* "Two Strong Hearts" (with Johnny Mathis)

1988: *Goya . . . a Life in Song,* "'Til I Loved You" (with Plácido Domingo), "Once a Time (I Loved You)"

1989: Quincy Jones, *Back on the Block,* "The Places You Find Love"

1989: Paul Anka, *Somebody Loves You,* "You and I" (with Paul Anka)

1990: *Dionne and Friends,* "Forever Friends"

1990: Melba Moore, *Soul Exposed,* "Lift Every Voice and Sing"

1990: *A Christmas Miracle, Vol. 1,* "O Holy Night"

1990: *Lifestyles of the Rich and Famous,* "Champagne Wishes and Caviar Dreams"

1991: Johnny Mathis, *Better Together: The Duet Album*, "Who's Counting Heartaches" (with Johnny Mathis)

1991: Gladys Knight, *Good Woman*, "Superwoman" (with Gladys Knight and Patti LaBelle)

1991: *Blue System*, "Déjà Vu" and "It's All Over" (with Dieter Bohlen)

1991: *A Christmas Miracle, Vol. 2*, "Winter Wonderland"

1992: Jose Augusto, *Jose Augusto, Quase Um Sonho*, "Almost a Dream" (with Jose Augusto)

1992: *Til Their Eyes Shine*, CD and video, "Sail Away" and "Dreamland"

1992: *The Best of James Bond*, debut of "Mr. Kiss Kiss Bang Bang" (recorded in 1965)

1992: *A Christmas Miracle, Vol. 3*, "It Came Upon a Midnight Clear"

1993: *Batacoto*, "Camaleao"

1994: *Celebration in Vienna* (with Plácido Domingo)

1994: *Miracle on 34th Street* original soundtrack "It's Beginning to Look a Lot Like Christmas"

1994: *Grammy's Greatest Moments, Vol. 4*, "I'll Never Love This Way Again" (live)

1995: Grace Bumbry, *With Love*, "Just Like a Woman" (with Grace Bumbry)

1996: Jazz Crusaders, *Louisiana Hot Sauce*, "Sweet Praline (When You're So Far Away)"

1997: B.B. King, *Deuces Wild*, "Hummingbird" (with B.B. King)

1997: Chuck Jackson, *I'll Never Get Over You*, "If I Let Myself Go" (with Chuck Jackson) in English, and "Si Me Dejo Llevar" (If I Let Myself Go) Spanish

1998: Burt Bacharach, *One Amazing Night*, "Walk On By," "I Say a Little Prayer" "Do You Know the Way to San Jose" (with Burt Bacharach) (live)

1998: Sacha Distel, *Sacha Distel: Ecoute Mes Yeux.* "Si l'On Pouvait Arrêter le Temps" (If We Could Stop Time) (with Sacha Distel)

1998: *Christmas Classic,* "White Christmas"

1998: *First Wives Club Soundtrack,* "Wives and Lovers"

1999: Burt Bacharach, *A Tribute to Burt Bacharach and Hal David at the Royal Albert Hall,* "Walk On By," "I Say a Little Prayer," "Do You Know the Way to San Jose," "Anyone Who Had a Heart," "What the World Needs Now" (with Burt Bacharach) (live)

1999: *Dionne Warwick and Friends: Divas of Soul,* recordings produced by Tony Camillo in 1973, released in 1999, "You Are a Song," "Best Thing That Ever Happened," "In Between the Heartaches," "Don't Say I Didn't Tell You So," "Loving You Is Just an Old Habit," "Seeing You Again," "The Need to Be"

1999: *Isn't She Great* original soundtrack, "On My Way"

1999: Cauby Peixoto, *Cauby Canta Sinatra,* "Where or When" (with Cauby Peixoto)

1999: *Happily Ever After: Fairy Tales for Every Child, The Bremen Town Musicians,* "Gonna Make It Big (in Bremen Town)" (with Gladys Knight, Jennifer Lewis, and George Clinton)

1999: *The Sissy Duckling,* "Time Takes Time"

2000: *Snow Boy Presents the Hi-Hat: The True Jazz Dance Sessions,* "Caravan"

2002: *All-Star Christmas at the Vatican,* "Adeste Fideles," "O Come All Ye Faithful," "White Christmas," and "Voice of Maria"

2002: Eduardo M Del Signore, *Captivated,* "Song of Ossanha"

2002: *Batacoto 3,* "Lua Candeia" (Moonlight)

2003: *Church: Songs of Soul and Inspiration,* "What the World Needs Now" (gospel version)

2003: *Jools Holland & His Rhythm and Blues Orchestra: More Friends,* "What Goes Around"

2003: Sacha Distel, *When I Fall in Love,* "Si l'On Pouvait Arrêter le Temps" (If We Could Stop Time), "When I Fall in Love," and "The Good Life" (with Sacha Distel)

2004: *Straight from the Heart,* PBS, CD, and DVD, "I'll Never Fall in Love Again," "What the World Needs Now," "Do You Know the Way to San Jose," "I'll Never Love This Way Again" (live)

2005: Mariella Nava, *Condivisioni,* "It's Forever" (with Mariella Nava) (anthem for the FIS Alpine World Ski Championships in Bormio)

2006: Cliff Richard, *Two's Company: The Duets,* "Anyone Who Had a Heart" (with Cliff Richard)

2007: *Daddy's Little Girls* motion picture soundtrack, "Family First" (with Whitney Houston, Cissy Houston, Dionne Warwick, Dee Dee Warwick, and family)

2008: Steve Tyrell, *Back to Bacharach,* "What the World Needs Now" (with an all-star cast)

2008: Ray Brown Jr., *Friends and Family,* "I Wish You Love" (with Ray Brown Jr.)

2009: *Mario Pelchat Chante Michel Legrand,* "How Do You Keep the Music Playing" (with Mario Pelchat and Michel Legrand)

Dionne Warwick
Selected Filmography

1964: *Thank Your Lucky Stars* TV (herself) (3 episodes 1964–1965)

1965: *Ready Steady Go!* TV (herself)

1965: *The Bacharach Sound* TV (herself)

1967: *The Red Skelton Hour* TV (herself)

1967: *The Merv Griffin Show* TV (herself)

1967: *The Joey Bishop Show* TV (herself)

1967: *Annual Academy Awards* TV (herself/performer)

1968: *The Beautiful Phyllis Diller Show* TV (herself)

1969: *Slaves* (movie)

1970: *Dean Martin Comedy Hour* TV (herself)

1970: *The Name of the Game,* "I Love You Billy Parker" (2 episodes)

1970: *Ed Sullivan Show* (5 episodes 1967–1970)

1972: *The Flip Wilson Show* TV (herself)

1973: *The Midnight Special* TV (herself)

1976: *Switch* (2 episodes)

1976: "The Original Rompin' Stompin' Hot and Heavy, Cool and Groovy All-Star Jazz Show" TV (host)

1977: *The Rockford Files*

1981: *Lou Rawls Parade of Stars* TV (herself)

1982: *Portrait of a Legend* (documentary)

1983: *All Star Party for Frank Sinatra* TV (herself)

1983: *George Burns Celebrates 80 Years in Show Business* TV (herself)

1983: *25th Annual Grammy Awards* TV (herself)

1985: *We Are the World* TV (herself)

1986: *The Fall Guy* TV

1986: *The Return of Mickey Spillane's Mike Hammer*

1986: *Sisters in the Name of Love* TV (herself)

1986: *28th Annual Grammy Awards* TV (herself)

1986: *Solid Gold,* host TV (5 episodes 1981–1986)

1987: "1st Annual Soul Train Music Awards" TV, host

1987: *Rent-a-Cop*

1988: "2nd Annual Soul Train Music Awards" TV, host

1988: "Aretha Franklin: The Queen of Soul" TV (herself)

1989: *Family Feud Challenge* TV (herself)

1990: "Sammy Davis Jr. 60th Anniversary Celebration" TV (herself)

1991: *Extralarge*

1991: *Dionne and Friends* (16 episodes), host

1991: *The Oprah Winfrey Show* TV (herself)

1992: "The 34th Annual Grammy Awards" TV (herself)

1993: *Out All Night*

1993: *Noche Noche*

1993: *Pop Goes Summer* (documentary)

1996: *Captain Planet and the Planeteers*

1996: *Wayans Brothers*

1996: "27th NAACP Image Awards" TV (herself)

1996: *American Masters: Lena Horne: In Her Own Words* TV (herself)

1997: *Pauly*

1997: *The Drew Carey Show* TV (herself)

1997: *King of the Hill*

1998: "Burt Bacharach: One Amazing Night" TV (herself)

1999: "Arista Records 25th Anniversary Celebration" TV (herself)

1999: *So Weird*

1998: *The Bold and the Beautiful*

1999: *Johnny Bravo*

2000: "72nd Annual Academy Awards" TV (herself/performer)

2000: *A&E Biography* (documentary)

2000: *Walker Texas Ranger*

2001: *Biography: Don't Make Me Over* TV (herself)

2001: "Michael Jackson: 30th Anniversary Celebration" TV (herself)

2002: "Christmas at the Vatican" (TV) herself

2002: *Lifetime: Intimate Portrait* (documentary) (herself)

2003: "Soul Man: Isaac Hayes" TV (herself)

2004: *Intimate Portrait* TV (herself)

2006: *The Dionne Warwick Story* (concert and documentary DVD set)

2006: *Celebrity Duets* TV (herself)

2006: *American Idol* TV (herself)

2006: "Legends Ball" TV (herself)

2007: *Dancing with the Stars* TV (herself)

2007: "Trumpets Awards" TV (herself)

2008: *Tavis Smiley* TV (herself)

2009: "Michael Jackson Memorial" TV (herself)

2009: "24th Annual Stellar Gospel Music Awards" TV (herself)

Dionne Warwick's discographies, film, and award lists courtesy of the Dionne Warwick Archive; the Dionne Warwick International Fan Club, Neil Barr, archivist; and in part from the Internet Movie Database (IMDb).

Index

Holiday, Billie, 93
Holland, Brian, 75
Holland, Eddie, 75
Hollywood Walk of Fame, 185, 199
Holmes, Richard "Groove," 57
Hope, Bob, 111, 135, 194
Hopper, Sean, 253
Horne, Lena, 39, 40, 66, 68, 94, 110,
    111, 127, 143, 149, 235, 254
House of Deréon, 185
"House Is Not a Home, A" (Bacharach
    and David), 47
Houston, Emily "Cissy" Drinkard (aunt),
    7–9, 13, 24, 39, 47, 99, 117, 118,
    120–22, 126, 155, 156, 221, 225–27
Houston, Gary (cousin), 117, 119, 121,
    225
Houston, John (Cissy's husband), 117,
    120–21
Houston, Michael (cousin), 117, 119
Houston, Whitney (cousin), 7, 90, 105,
    110, 117–27, 130, 170, 210, 225–27
Howard, Miki, 134
Howard Theater (Washington, D.C.), 34
"How Can You Mend a Broken Heart"
    (Gibb brothers), 102
"How Deep Is Your Love" (Gibb brothers),
    102
"How Many Times Can We Say Goodbye"
    (Vandross), 130
"How Will I Know" (Merrill and
    Rubicam), 122
Humperdinck, Engelbert, 52, 98
Hunt, Tommy, 14, 18, 19, 43
Hunter, Todd, 248, 252

I

"I Believe in Christmas" (song), 215
Ice Cube, 179
Ice-T, 179
"I Don't Want to Cry" (Jackson), 97
"I Just Called to Say I Love You"
    (Wonder), 139, 140
"I Just Don't Know What to Do with
    Myself" (Bacharach and David), 43
"I Know I'll Never Love This Way Again"
    (Kerr and Jennings), 89, 133–34
"I'll Never Fall in Love Again" (Bacharach
    and David), 44–45
I Look to You (album), 126

Imam, 254
"I Met Him on a Sunday" (Shirelles), 19
"I'm Gonna Make You Love Me"
    (Gamble, Huff, and Ross), 223
Imperials, the, 14
Ingram, James, 90, 253
Integrated Marketing Communication
    (IMC), 188
International Hotel (Las Vegas), 67, 101
Interscope Records, 182
"I Say a Little Prayer" (Bacharach and
    David), 43, 132
Isley Brothers, the, 19, 210
"I Smiled Yesterday" (Bacharach and
    David), 21
"It's Love That Really Counts" (Bacharach
    and David), 18
"It's Not Unusual" (Reed and Mills), 98
"I've Got You Where I Want You" (song),
    129
"I Want to Be with You" (Adams and
    Strouse), 223
"I Will Always Love You" (Parton), 123

J

Jackson, Chuck, 14, 18, 19, 31–32, 52,
    97, 98, 223
Jackson, Curtis, 186–87
Jackson, Don, 136
Jackson, Freddie, 134
Jackson, Helen, 97
Jackson, Jackie, 253
Jackson, Janet, 254
Jackson, Jermaine, 134
Jackson, La Toya, 253
Jackson, Mahalia, 9, 37
Jackson, Marlon, 253
Jackson, Michael, 104, 127, 235, 253
Jackson, Pam, 93
Jackson, Randy, 253
Jackson, Tito, 253
Jamison, Judith, 254
Jamison, Mechalie, 184
Jarreau, Al, 130, 253
Jay and the Americans, 35
Jay-Z, 186
Jennings, Waylon, 253
"Jesus Loves Me" (Warner and Bradbury),
    1–2, 221, 239
Jet magazine, 135, 202